June 22, 1984

Richard Estes, *Drugstore*
Collection of The Art Institute of Chicago
Courtesy of: Richard Estes and Allan Stone Gallery

THE SELF-APPARENT WORD

Fiction as Language / Language as Fiction

Jerome Klinkowitz

Southern Illinois University Press / Carbondale and Edwardsville

Library of Congress Cataloging in Publication Data

Klinkowitz, Jerome.
  The self-apparent word.

  Includes index.
    1. American fiction—20th century—History and criticism. I. Title.
PS379.K553 1984   813'.54'09   83-20071
ISBN 0-8093-1164-X

Grateful acknowledgment is extended to the authors and
Fiction Collective for permission to quote from Steve
Katz, *Moving Parts*, copyright © 1977 by Steve Katz
(New York: Fiction Collective, 1977), and Clarence Ma-
jor, *Reflex and Bone Structure*, copyright © 1975 by Clar-
ence Major (New York: Fiction Collective, 1975).

Edited by Stephen W. Smith
Designed by David Ford
Production supervised by Kathy Giencke
87 86 85 84   4 3 2 1

For Richard Kostelanetz

CONTENTS

PREFACE

The Self-Apparent Word is the third panel in a triptych, providing
the theory to accompany my literary history, *Literary Disruptions*
(Urbana: University of Illinois Press, 1975, revised 1980), and
my cultural survey, *The American 1960s* (Ames: Iowa State University Press, 1980). All three books argue that there exists a
definite style of innovative writing, flourishing since the
mid-1960s, which challenges the most basic conventions of fiction. In my previous studies this challenge was described as a
general attack on the suspension of disbelief: the new fiction
would not represent the world but rather be something made
and added to it. In preparing a theory to fully describe this development, I have chosen to replace the negatively phrased sense
of anti-illusionism with the more positive term "self-apparency,"
for it is my belief that the revolution we have witnessed in
American fiction is a more constructive affair. To avoid creating
an obscure jargon, I've tried to limit my terminology of theory
to obvious concepts generated by the styles of fiction themselves:
"self-effacing" words of traditional fiction draw little attention
to themselves as they work as transparent windows upon the
world their stories represent, whereas "self-apparent" words are
more opaque, forcing the reader to attend to the form of trans-
mission (where the story's action now takes place).

Sole support for all my work over the past decade and a half has come from the University of Northern Iowa. Careful readings of the manuscript were given by Ronald Sukenick, Raymond Federman, James Justus, Jack Hicks, and Richard Kostelanetz. As always, Julie Huffman-klinkowitz contributed her active help. Walter Abish helped straighten out my title and clarify my thinking on fictive self-apparency. Editors Robley Wilson (*The North American Review*) and Maurice Couturier (*La Représentation et la performance dans la fiction postmoderne*) were receptive to my first thoughts on experimental realism, as were audiences at Fordham, Duke, and the Université de Nice. I am especially grateful to Maurice Couturier and Marc Chénetier for hosting my visits to France, and to Malcolm Bradbury, Chris Bigsby, and Bill Buford for their hospitality during my stays in England where this book was completed.

London   JEROME KLINKOWITZ
July 1983

THE SELF-APPARENT WORD

chapter 1 INTRODUCTION

Let's begin with the simplest and most traditional of narratives: a love story. Two characters proceed along lines of development which at a certain point intersect. For a time, their love keeps them together on closely parallel tracks, and their two life stories are one. But all readers know that eventually these lines will separate, if only with the death of one character. Every story begins with the promise of its end; for every life a death, for every act of love a moment of heartbreak. Such is the emotion of fictional narrative.

But there are different ways to tell a love story, key differences which indicate a fundamental divergence in one's approach to literary art. In the traditional manner, a novelist can write a love story with his or her emphasis on what happens to the characters as they experience the narrative's routines. Frank Norris' *Mc-Teague* (1899) is an extreme example, thanks to the author's philosophical commitment to a theory of literary naturalism which saw individuals as determined by overwhelming social and biological forces—the very experiences, in other words, of their love. Mac loves Trina, even though the affair is a mismatch of an oversized brute with a dainty and meticulous little miser. There are other obstacles to their love which must be overcome: Mac's rival, Marcus, and a lack of money with which to begin a household. Yet even as these problems are resolved with a great deal of surface fussiness and adventure, deeper concerns make themselves felt. Mac's simple sensuosity conflicts with Trina's more abstract, intellectual nature. The course of their love affair founders: Trina scrimps and saves to hide the family's income, while Mac berates and beats her. Natural forces drive them from their parallel paths, until their divergence is graphic. Hiding her gold to the last, Trina is murdered by Mac who then sets out across the wilderness, pursued by a vengeful Marcus who traps him at the center of Death Valley. No one survives—an extreme completion of the circle which began at the fated moment when Mac and Trina first met.

The generating force of *McTeague*, therefore, is *self-effacing*: the couple's love affair becomes less apparent than the kaleidoscope of activity which results from it. Their meeting, in other words, is an excuse for something else, and once that liaison begins the reader's attention is directed to the external display of *what happens next*. Once the obstacles to their union are removed, the device of their relationship becomes self-effacing; that Mac loves Trina and Trina loves Mac can be forgotten, as their affection is overwhelmed by the monstrosities of plot which follow.

And so the essence of this most fundamental of narrative fictions operates by contradiction: the lovers' meeting is absolutely essential to generate Norris' story, but once they do meet the creative force of their relationship disappears before the play of events it engenders. What would happen if, however so fated, the lovers never actually met within the story, but simply kept impending toward that inevitable meeting throughout the author's text? This simple shift in strategy would turn the essentials of fiction around, replacing the self-effacing words of represented events with a more concrete self-apparency of form. The lovers' meeting would be a thing in itself, perfectly opaque rather than transparent as technique, from which all else, being inevitable, could be implied.

This transposition supplies the form for Raymond Federman's *Moinous & Sucette (a love story of sorts)*,[1] a novel in which the full story of a couple's relationship is told without their ever meeting. The narrative begins with a close encounter on a late winter afternoon in New York's Washington Square where the two "almost meet, when they are both in the same place at the same time."

But that day, they do not speak. No. They smile at one another. Nothing more. A fleeting complicitous smile, as if they already know that they are destined to meet again.

Even though the future lovers do not meet in Washington Square, there is action between them as figures in Federman's text, because there is

reason, therefore, to mention this initial encounter across a smile, even though Moinous & Sucette do not really meet and speak that day. But they do come face to face, and that should be noted, for later, when they will reach the peak of their passionate relationship, they will often recall that twinkle of perception, that impromptu eye contact, and the smile they exchanged as a sign of future connivance. (P. 7)

In a conventional love story, that signal of relationship would be at once incorporated into the represented narrative action—it would become effaced, in other words, before the presentational aspect of the story. But in Federman's text it retains its power as a sign—the lovers can themselves later look back to it as a moment in the book—and therefore is more apparent as a thing in itself, an object made and added to the world just as it figures as an icon in the lovers' own story of their relationship.

Federman amplifies this technique by giving the reader more and more details about Moinous' and Sucette's lives, particularly as they relate to their impending meeting; but to keep these signals of character self-apparent, he never lets them actually meet. With the action located in his text rather than on the projected screen of narrative activity, he can take the time to dally with the finer points of setting and tone, such as a rainy day, for it "always rains in sad love stories." The abortive meeting can be run and rerun through Federman's text, because it is generating its own time of hypothetical composition, like a painter slowly filling in details, rather than being dependent upon a narrative whose action has been set loose from the page. Therefore its sense becomes sharpened even as it doesn't happen. The reader's imaginative picture of each character is thus completed and refined without benefit of distracting action. "His hair, the crease in his pants, the leftover reflexes from the army, his dislike of rain, these may seem like minor details, but revealing, revealing indeed" (p. 8).

Without any loss of human interest or concern, Federman has shifted the reader's attention from the action of a story taking place to the action of a text being composed; the words are self-apparent, not self-effacing. Surprisingly, the characters grow deeper thanks to this technique. Moinous' loneliness as an expatriate can be viewed more sympathetically as we see how deeply he needs someone like Sucette, even as their impending meeting is delayed. "The soul of a displaced person is an empty region which cannot be approached or explored" (p. 9), as any realistic writer would admit; therefore Federman's approach must be a matter of indirection, like glancing askance to sense the brilliance of a comet.

This lingering sense of deferral complements Federman's theme of alienated hopes in America's promised land. In each of his previous novels—*Double or Nothing* (1971), *Take It or Leave It* (1976), *The Voice in the Closet* (1979), and *The Twofold Vibration* (1982)—the author had taken the character of a young French immigrant much like himself and created a narrative of hope and expectation, foiled at each point of development by the pragmatic facts of life. Each of these novels depended upon a movement of sorts, whether the character's efforts to arrange the logistics of his year's writing-time or this same person's trip across the United States. But in *Moinous & Sucette* Federman shows that the device of never letting his lovers meet complements his usual theme: "And America," as Moinous is gradually and painfully discovering, "is a land where the impact of disillusion is spent in advance," just as every detail of his meeting with Sucette will be given full textual play before the event itself happens. "A land of transparent duplication of old feelings and restless gestures" (p. 9). Moinous is alone with his memories, which remain locked in the novel's text until he can meet Sucette and tell her his story. She, meanwhile, feels estranged from her solidly American heritage, which her Boston-bred parents can trace back to the *Mayflower*. Involved in radical causes and a bohemian lifestyle, she herself can find expression in her solitude only by taking a creative writing class and writing a story which sums up her own feelings for life. Before she forms a close relationship with Moinous in life, she fantasizes him as a character in her fiction; thus each of the principal actors in Federman's antinarrative creates his or her own text in advance of playing it out in life, allowing readers to examine all feelings and motives in their fictional state before the flow of life ever has a chance (as it does so soon in *McTeague*) to sweep these subtleties away.

Federman's text is its own reality, complementing the philosophical belief that the past and future are illusions with only the present moment as real. Since both of his characters are "in a state of emotional availability, anything can happen"—the text is perfectly alive and open. "Except that neither of them can anticipate the consequences of their love story. Isn't that always the case?" (p. 22). As his novel's first chapter concludes, Federman warns the reader not to worry for the inevitability of his characters fate: true, they are determined to part, but if he never lets them meet their viability will exist forever.

The beginning of every story, writes Kafka, is ridiculous at first. There seems no hope that this newborn thing, still incomplete and tender in every joint, will be able to keep alive in the completed organization of the world, which, like every completed organization, strives to close itself off. However, one should not forget that the story, if it has any justification to exist, bears its complete organization within itself even before it has been fully formed. For this reason despair over the beginning of a story is unwarranted. (P. 27)

Moinous & Sucette draws its strength from the continuous present of this first vital moment, which is sustained by "the rigamarole of contrariety" surrounding it in life. As opposed to fiction in which signs become transparent and lose their sense of identity, Federman's text capitalizes on language's function as a system of differences to keep these signs in play, deferring any final sense of meaning. Once a story begins, the reader's rush to meaning virtually closes the book; therefore *Moinous & Sucette* is suspended in its state of perfect immanence, remaining fictive to the end.

There are, of course, fictions more complex than Norris' or Federman's. But as with their choice of either self-effacing or self-apparent strategies, these more discursive works can go either way.

Once it is determined that two characters will meet, a history of their relationship develops. For Norris and for Federman, in their opposite ways, this history becomes an open-and-shut case—in *McTeague* a result of the inexorable determination of naturalistic biological and sociological forces, while in *Moinous & Sucette* a consequence of their affair existing completely in hypothesis. There is a different tactic available to the novelist, of which E. L. Doctorow's *Ragtime*, Ishmael Reed's *Yellow Back Radio Broke Down*, and Steve Katz' *Moving Parts* are contrasting examples. Attention can be directed to the history of the novel's action, in these cases by shifting attention from the characters as identities to their play of signification (what their identities imply for the novel's action).

Ragtime[2] has no central characters. Instead, no sooner is one person's home introduced than it becomes lost in the swirl of action—both of the novel's fictive events and the context of world history transpiring at this same time of 1902. Far from being the novel's mere setting, this conflux of activity suggests the pervasive aspect of human effort, whether political (such as Teddy Roosevelt's presidency) or artistic. "This was the time in our history," the narrator reminds us, "when Winslow Homer was doing his painting. A certain light was still available along the Eastern seaboard. Homer painted the light" (p. 4). There is also, in retrospect (and *Ragtime* is most definitely a retrospective book, a grandfatherly confession to the present age), a certain quality of evolving action which not only locates the novel in history but defines the character of the times. "The painters in Paris were doing portraits with two eyes on one side of the head. A Jewish professor in Zurich had published a paper proving that the universe was curved" (p. 259). Tenative connections abound, as Harry Houdini, Harry K. Thaw, Emma Goldman, Scott Joplin, and J. P. Morgan keep bumping into each other amid the twists of Doctorow's plot. Although there is the temptation to read this novel as a melange of fiction and history, the historical has not yet gained that status, as all is still in flux—the world of 1902 is just being invented, as is Doctorow's novel, and for the time each is provisional. There can be mix-ups, as when the Archduke Franz Ferdinand greets Houdini as the inventor of the airplane, or as when it is rumored that Thomas Edison's latest invention is a vacuum tube which lets him talk with the dead. History in *Ragtime* exists just at the point of its own making; Jacob Riis encounters the pathetic life of slum dwellers a page after the reader has seen it firsthand. Simple action precedes both history and fiction, as when Evelyn Nesbit appears at the trial of Harry K. Thaw and "her testimony created the first sex goddess in American history," providing "the inspiration for the concept of the movie star system for every sex goddess from Theda Bara to Marilyn Monroe" (pp. 70, 71). As in Federman's *Moinous & Sucette*, action is in free play, able to go either way of fantasy or fact; all is tentative, and it is an open contest as to who gets top billing in the history books, Peary discovering the North Pole or Houdini making one more impossible escape.

Doctorow's *Ragtime* hovers between apparency and effacement. History is an actor rather than established event, but because its readers from this late vantage know which way the action went, its effacement as chronicle eventually subsumes its apparency as fictive act. *Ragtime*'s final effect is one of transparent narration, with only occasional moments of opaque apparency which, as with Edison's talking with the dead, stick out like sore thumbs. The reader is encouraged to partake of novelty, either reading fiction as history or history as fiction, but in either case the novel's makings efface themselves before the story being told. The artist's transcendent play of signifiers is quickly brought to earth, with each sign firmly anchored to what it conventionally signifies. *Ragtime* is noted for its level, almost emphatically flat tone, as both the familiar and the marvelous are paraded before the reader in the same deadpan language. The narrative moves at one speed, like the incessancy of a ragtime piano accompaniment to a Keystone scenario. The language of its creation disappears before the spectacle of its created product.

Just the opposite effect is achieved by Ishmael Reed in *Yellow Back Radio Broke Down*.[3] In this novel the mixture of imagination and fact do not so much tell a story as generate a language. History is never allowed to subsume fantasy because the combination continually draws attention to itself by slapstick anachronisms and self-conscious delight in the weird spectacle produced. For all its daring invention, *Ragtime* presents nothing that is not possible—in the end, it is an illusionistic work. But rather than combine various elements from a single time period, as does Doctorow, Reed mixes the time periods themselves; rather than providing a context for his fiction, historical events are allowed in collage manner to be themselves at the very same time they are combined; only the artist's act can combine them, as in the natural course of events they could never possibly meet. Because the components of Reed's fiction are anti-illusionistic, the action of his story takes place in the language of narration. Its very first lines, "Folks. This here is the story of the Loop Garoo

Kid," introduce within its very language the three levels of anachronistic mixture, combining the Wild West with voodoo and modern technology: "A cowboy so bad he made a working posse of spells phone in sick" (p. 9). The narrative has all the fittings of a cowboy tale, including towns and taverns, but their names—"Video Junction" and "Big Lizzie's Rabid Black Cougar Saloon"—draw attention back to the author's composition. Language is never wasted; nothing is effaced. Even a random notation of the stock Western scene of ominous foreboding, such as vultures circling above, is an occasion for poetic display. "In the distance large birds with buzzard coupons could be seen lining up for mess" (p. 33). When the chief bad man's gang chickens out, Reed sees the chance for another anachronistic metaphor, drawing attention to the immense gap between tenor and vehicle. "The cowpokes were pretending to be in a dentist's office of the mind," he writes. "They had their heads buried in magazines" (p. 117). When action does occur, it is on the level of symbol rather than of reality, as when Loop Garoo's voodoo is challenged by the pope himself (who speaks in a corny twentieth-century immigrant Italian, as if he is being played by Chico Marx).

Reed's use of history, then, is more technically self-conscious than is Doctorow's; his aim is less to tell a story than to create a new form of language from which the elements of narrative may be derived. The conventional process of realistic event building into myth is reversed so that the process itself may be appreciated, much as Robert Coover plays with the materials of American mythology (from comic books to history volumes) in *The Public Burning* (1977). But beyond this self-consciousness of language lies the fiction-making impulse itself, which Steve Katz makes his subject in *Moving Parts*,[4] a four-part exploration of all aspects of creating a story. First comes the imaginative experience, the author meeting his fantasy just as the two lovers meet (or almost meet) in the novels by Frank Norris and Raymond Federman. As a combination of journal, auctorial commentary, and conventionally narrated fiction, "Female Skin" examines all the aspects of this confrontation between an actual writer and his imaginary material. "These journal entries don't give us a sense of Wendy Appel," Katz realizes after a first start in each mode, "but they do embarrass me by making me recall what it was like to be enveloped by her" (p. 15). Wendy is the video film-maker Katz has met on location, and to show how he has been captivated by her he fashions several styles of narrative: journal entries, commentary, photographs, a signed legal release, and ultimately a short story. The last of these conveys the best sense of Wendy's influence, even though its actions are absurdly impossible. "I made the first incision at 7:15 A.M.," this story matter-of-factly begins. "It was an important step. I touched the point in lightly just under the left armpit and slowly pulled the blade down along her side" (p. 3). By the next page, the narrator is literally "in her skin," and the fiction is on its way to animating this old cliché.

Employing a deliberately flat language to describe an extraordinary event calls attention to both process and product; as Hemingway noted half a century ago, there is no hysteria which might interfere with the process of communication. But Hemingway wrote of real wars and wounds, while Katz is dealing in ridiculous fantasy, which highlights the precision of his language all the more. The story itself takes shape from this buffoonery: once enveloped in Wendy's skin, the narrator sets off for a walk around New York City, during which he attracts a huge flock of geese which take over the mayor's mansion. What this disruption has to do with Wendy Appel is apparent only by algebraic implication, for the geese's mysterious appearance and behavior bear the same relation to reality as does meeting Wendy Appel to the normal course of events.

"Parcel of Wrists," separately paginated, is the second section of *Moving Parts*, and is more of a self-contained story—though there is an important confrontation between author and narrative which sets up the following section (also individually paginated) titled "Trip." "In the morning's mail I received a parcel postmarked from Irondale, Tennessee," the story begins, as banal an invitation as "the Marquis went out at five o'clock" but richly potential nevertheless; from such small kernals may fantastic fictions emerge. What's in the package? "It was packed from top to bottom with human wrists," Happily, as in "Female Skin," there is no physical unpleasantness. Instead, actions and attitude are kept flatly emotionless so that the author can attend to the story's real business: "the strange detour my life had taken as a result of opening the morning mail" (p. 3).

The central part of "Parcel of Wrists" features the narrator's trip to Irondale, Tennessee, in search of the wrists' sender. Less interesting than the opening section, its relative lack of color leads the narrator to doubt whether he received the package at all; wondering whether it was all a dream, he hurries back to New York, where he verifies the wrists' existence and (again concretizing a metaphor) plants them to see how they sprout and bloom.

> I could describe them forever. Some grew in clusters, some singly, some drooped, some erect. One of the flowers was made of insects, tiny grey-golden flies clustered around a stem like lupine or larkspur, that scattered when you got close, the flower seeming to disappear in a scintillation of these little flies, then reappearing when you withdrew. One that looked like Indian paintbrush would curl itself around your finger as if you tried to touch it. Another, like a small peony, would lean toward you as you got close, and seem to pucker up as if it had the urge to give you a kiss. Each flower was a different color; not just a shade, but a distinct color.

As opposed to the hueless and inconsequential trip to Irondale, the wrists themselves—unexplained except as an occasion for wonder—now justify themselves as material for fiction. "My mind now is full of ten thousand colors," the narrator exclaims, "colors that are nowhere visible, that even Fra Angelico could never have touched to canvas" (p. 29).

Confident of his writer's ability and anxious to see how it

matches up to hard core reality, Katz embarks on the third of
the moving parts of his narrative, "Trip," in which he decides to
"move on from the condition of being Steve Katz to assume the
guise of the personal pronoun 'he,' the Protagonist" (p. 10).
Having fully imagined both Irondale, Tennessee, and the parcel
of wrists mailed from it, he boards a Nashville-bound bus to see
just how reality may or may not correspond with his fiction.
Having controlled events through the "Parcel" story, he now encounters a diffidence in his writing.

> Iron City as it is on its small hill brushes through his life for a few
> moments like a coming attraction, a few curtains parted, situated
> in its own integrity, a ripeness of itself just where it is, no fiction
> after all, but a place in its place, tended by its people. He feels too
> shy to violate it. (P. 30).

Making himself a protagonist invites a general fictionality of experience. "He spent the night on Broadway unravelling from
honky-tonk to honky-tonk just like in the songs" (p. 31), en-
countering poetry "for free" in the massage-parlor pitches.
Reaching Iron City, a place he had previously invented from maps
and perceptions, he finds no hardness of fact. "Its reality for me
seems extremely delicate, as every assumption of reality becomes
fragile" (p. 45). What would otherwise be a solidly real yet banally unaffective place becomes shockingly personal by virtue of
Katz' imaginative relationship to it—a metaphor for an enrich-
ing way of dealing with the world at large. Once this status is
achieved, there is no need to keep inventing, as the artist's invention takes over with its own momentum.

> The place is so precise in its own equilibrium of lives, so perfect in
> its virginal decay, that I don't want to ripple the surface at all, or
> drop the weight of my fiction into the real time of this place, alter-
> ing their time even if only slightly. (P. 47)

Caught between its reality and his own fiction, Katz learns that
in this state of suspension truth will exist only "as resonances"
in "the art of telling" (p. 74). "Art prepares the bed of contin-

gencies from which reality sprouts, ripens, and is harvested" (p. 75), since nothing can be said to exist until the imagination has made it personally relevant.

The exact nature of these resonances is the subject of the most ambitious and intellectually challenging of the moving parts, "43." The title refers to Katz' lucky number which through his life keeps popping up in surprising but seemingly inevitable ways. It codifies his belief that "design was everything, the 'whole thing,' 'where it was all at.' . . . the perfect image of an old truth, that the intricate surface of reality originates in and depends upon a singular mystery" (p. 3). The odd intersections of fantasy and fact had been the subject of "Trip," but now he is ready to propose a theory which explains these odd but seductive match-ups such as occasionally present themselves through astrology, the tarot, and other occult devices.

> These systems are tools useful to help you yourself arrive at a description of reality, but as soon as you depend upon the system itself for the answers, start looking *at* it rather than *through* it, there begins to form a cataract of dogma over your perception of things as they are. (P. 22)

This is what happened when Katz as protagonist tried to ground his fantasy of Irondale in Iron City, Tennessee. Fiction's great advantage over reality is that it offers comfort without proof, just the sense of confidence one needs to be at home in the world.

> It does seem relaxing to find that one of these systems works for us, because suddenly certain of our responsibilities for ourselves are taken off our heads for the moment, and we can give up some anxieties and get high. (P. 23)

Fiction allows one to be both within and beyond the world. "The most informed and exhilarating moments occur," Katz argues, "when quotidian reality and my inventions intersect or have a mutual resonance"; at these points "the real road becomes the fictional road, the fantastic and the real suddenly seem to come alive together and embrace the hours of my life with happy and mysterious affirmation" (p. 45).

In this manner Katz' *Moving Parts* both practices and explains the virtues of self-apparency. Self-effacing and self-apparent fiction provide the extremes of reading experience, but they are not polar opposites, for the latter includes the former (while not vice versa). The dual vision that self-apparency allows is a key to this form's fascination, and Donald Barthelme has made it the subject of his early story, "Me and Miss Mandible."[5] "Miss Mandible wants to make love to me but she hesitates because I am officially a child," the story begins—a complementary, Kafka-esque version of Katz' encounter with the morning's mail. *Something does not quite match up*, Barthelme's opening sentence signals; and exploring the comedy and insight of this disjunctiveness will be his story's strategy. The situation is starkly elemental: a thirty-five-year-old man has been inexplicably returned to the sixth grade, where he squirms uneasily among a class of eleven-year-olds awash in periripening sexuality. "My own allegiance, at the moment," the narrator confesses, "is divided between Miss Mandible and Sue Ann Brownly, who sits across the aisle from me all day long and is, like Miss Mandible, a fool for love" (p. 97). The contrast is between the narrator's vast experience (he has been an insurance adjustor, and has witnessed the world wrecked several times over) and the children's borderline innocence. Some can read the "Eddie and Debby" headlines from romance and screen magazines and know what they signify; other's can't. "Everything is promised my classmates and I, most of all the future," Barthelme's narrator notes. "We accept the outrageous assurances without blinking" (p. 107).

"Me and Miss Mandible" dramatizes the differences between self-effacing readings of the world (which the children practice) and the narrator's sense of apparency. "Plucked from my unexamined life among other pleasant, desperate, money-making young Americans, thrown backward in space and time, I am beginning to understand how I went wrong, how we all go wrong," he admits (p. 108). But his self-insight is less dramatic than his advantage over the children's inability to judge the world's sign-making system. "We read signs as promises," he observes, as Miss Mandible and Sue Ann each draw their own conclusions from his extraordinary presence, just as he himself had lived by the promise of his insurance company's motto.

> I believed that because I had obtained a wife who was made up of wife-signs (beauty, charm, softness, perfume, cookery) I had found love. Brenda, reading the same signs that have now misled Miss Mandible and Sue Ann Brownly, felt she had been promised that she would never be bored again. All of us, Miss Mandible, Sue Ann, myself, Brenda, Mr. Goodykind, still believe that the American flag betokens a kind of general righteousness.
>
> But I say, looking about me in this incubator of future citizens, that signs are signs, and that some of them are lies. This is the great discovery of my time here. (P. 109)

This too is the discovery of self-apparent fiction: *signs are signs, and some of them are lies.* The signifying process is not always direct, and signifiers do not always yield a transparent vision of the signified object. In the following chapter fiction which capitalizes on this ambiguity will be contrasted with the more traditional styles of narrative self-effacement. The history of twentieth-century literature has been one of steady progress toward self-apparency, and these various strategies will be studied in chapter 3. An intellectual form of adjustment is found in reflexive fiction, detailed in chapter 4; but the purest forms of self-apparency do not require the mechanics of an author writing about an author writing a story, and these provide the substance of chapter 5. How these techniques flow back into the mainstream and reinvent literary realism for our new anti-illusionistic times is discussed in the concluding chapter. Sociologists have described the current era as "the time of the sign." Since the social turmoils of the American 1960s and the similar aesthetic disruptions within fiction,[6] writing and reading habits have been readjusted, with more attention now given to the process of literary creation and less to the projected product. Self-apparency is more than a metaphor for this practice. It is the technique by which fiction makes evident its own creation. With the suspension of disbelief now suspended, readers may attend to the ultimate realism of words on the page and signs at play.

chapter 2   THE SELF-EFFACING WORD

The language of fiction has always been transparent, particularly
in the novel. Though some contemporary critics challenge naïve
realism by insisting that telling stories is just one of many things
fiction can do—and that early novelists such as Diderot, Rabelais, Sterne, and Smollet did much else with their art besides
spin out sequential narratives—even the developing novel sought
a framework which effaced the textuality of its words. *Jacques le
fataliste* and *Pantagruel* were received as works of philosophy and
satire; the verbal objects of each are read for what they say about
other objects in the real world, whether persons, places, and
things (Diderot) or virtues, vices, and attitudes (Rabelais). The
English novel, from Henry Fielding to Margaret Drabble, has
held fast to its narrative framework, the suspension-of-disbelief
in a once-upon-a-time reality being represented—a rigidly mimetic disposition somewhat like the earliest films which bolted
down the camera at front-row center because "the public won't
pay a nickel to see half an actor" (nor could a theatergoer be
expected to change one's seat as the action turned alternately
intimate or expansive).

As film was for a time inhibited by the conventions of an only
superficially sister art, drama, so has fiction had its opportuni-

ties trimmed by its likeness to news from the world. Even in *Tristram Shandy* with all its attention to style, there is never any doubt that a "real story" is being told. And even before the conventional notion of storytelling as a trustworthy form was established by Fielding, Samuel Richardson thought the public would read a novel only if it could believe in the legitimacy of its existence—in this case the evidence of letters exchanged among the characters.

The first transparency, then, is form, whether of snooping into a bundle of correspondence, listening to an artfully told story (allegedly true or not), or participating in a counterfeit of history itself. It is difficult for language to be self-apparent when its reason for being is a duplicate of something already functional in society. Whether symbol or sign, medieval or modern, fiction sacrifices its own formal identity to the world's ideology. "Poetry is made of words, not ideas," Mallarmé argued during the aesthetic revolution which released that genre from obligations to tell stories, dramatize, moralize, or instruct; that fiction lagged a hundred years behind is due in part to the condescending excuses made, from the very start, for its being. That the words of fiction have meant something else besides their mundane significations, and that works written and received under a mimetic dispensation can be reinterpreted today as self-apparent language, does not mean a revolution in form has not taken place. Substances and forms may exist simultaneously in the same objects, as Ferdinand de Saussure has shown: the 8:25 P.M. Geneva-to-Paris Express is thought to be the same train each day, even though one can visualize it only as the physical collection of a locomotive, certain cars, and a particular crew which is in fact different for each journey. Where one's imagination is channeled, in reading both train schedules and novels, determines how the words are read: as formal indicators or as objects in themselves.

Saussure's distinction in linguistics is vaguely paralleled by other revolutions of thought in physics, mathematics, and the sciences in general—all part of the general twentieth-century transformation away from the stable content of a thing in itself and toward the new notion of relativity. Indeed, much twentieth-century thought has worked for the overthrow of nineteenth-century notions of realism. But the last to surrender has been that of literary verisimilitude, and as late as the 1960s, 70s, and 80s fictions could be written which employed either the axioms of effacement or apparency in language. Different philosophical world views stand behind each manner of treatment; far from being mere techniques, the use of either self-effacing or self-apparent words implies a judgment as to the nature of experience. That such competing fictions could be written side by side indicates the ambiguous status of contemporary fiction. Two excellent examples are Philip Roth's novella *Goodbye, Columbus*[1] and Kurt Vonnegut's "The Hyannis Port Story."[2] Each is addressed to the mainstream of American culture, though it is ironic that the more conservative of the two, Roth's novella, actually appeared in a more intellectually *chic* magazine (*Paris Review*, as opposed to Vonnegut's intended market of the *Saturday Evening Post*). Read together, they pose the question of whether their fictions more properly exist as themselves, or for what they represent.

Philip Roth's novella *Goodbye, Columbus* depicts a world whose coherence, stability, and order precede Einstein, Heisenberg and Gödel. The fact that its depiction of the social world would be discernable to readers of Charles Dickens' day yet also remains pertinent and entertaining to contemporary audiences suggests that, as far as any common man or woman cares, the great revolutions of physics and philosophy need not have taken place. What makes this work utterly traditional, however, is its transparency of language. Beyond each word stands an object in the real world, and it is the manipulation of those worldly objects rather than language on the page which forms the author's art. The world described could be relative, uncertain, or indeterminate; the key to Roth's art is that he is conducting a pantomime with signified objects rather than using words in and for themselves.

Indeed, the worlds (and there are distinctly two of them) described in *Goodbye, Columbus* defy most principles of order. In urban Newark, where the narrator lives with relatives, chaos seems the rule, even at dinnertime. "None of us ate together: my Aunt Gladys ate at five o'clock, my cousin Susan at five-thirty, me at six, and my uncle at six-thirty. There is nothing to explain this beyond the fact that my aunt is crazy" (p. 2). Meanwhile, in the wealthy suburb of Short Hills (where the narrator is about to find a new girlfriend), dinner is served amidst a different order of confusion, as the family members sit together but maintain a half dozen separate conversations at once. But in both cases pantomimes of human activity are the objects, which in their very confusion are contrast to the approved social norm (which is, in turn, the implicit structure for *Goodbye, Columbus*, just as determining as Samuel Richardson's letters or Henry Fielding's storytelling pose). The narrative identifies objects from this common social structure, such as each family's refrigerator (source of food; sign of behavior; symbol of values), and uses them as cues for reader response. For example, Aunt Gladys harries her family with a refrigerator stocked with the opposites of what they want, everything about to spoil and under orders to be eaten at once. "I only hope she dies with an empty refrigerator," we are told, "otherwise she'll ruin eternity for everyone else, what with her Velveeta turning green, and her navel oranges growing fuzzy jackets down below" (p. 7). Meanwhile, out in Short Hills, the wealthy Patimkin family owns a spare refrigerator—the old one from their poorer Newark days now kept in the recreation room and stocked with a cornucopia of luxurious fruits far too plentiful ever to be eaten.

Two refrigerators, two families, two utterly different life-styles and values to support them—Roth's objects are rich in their associations, signifying to the reader an entire world of character and theme. But the refrigerators have done their job as physical

objects, as signs themselves for their culture, rather than as signifiers kept within the bounds of language. There is a one-to-
one correspondence between Aunt Gladys' icebox and the reader's attitudes it summons; the process is so rigid and automatic
that any sense of the "poetic" in language, as Roman Jakobson
has put it, is effaced. There is no meaning supplementary to the
normative signifying line, nothing charged with instinctual drives
or even nuances, no material existing independently of the sign.
It is all denotation. For truly poetic or fictive language, "The
word is experienced as word and not as a simple substitute for a
named object," Jakobson claims;[3] yet the language of *Goodbye,
Columbus* does all its work as a substitute for real objects—refrigerators, makes of automobiles, neighborhoods, and income
levels—which themselves function as signs within society.

The entire substance of *Goodbye, Columbus* can be codified in
its network of object-signs, all of which dictate an unambiguous
response. The social and economic contrasts between the two
families is dramatized in object-laden gestures, such as the narrator's aunt packing him a homely bag lunch for the Patimkins'
lavish garden party. The theme of Jews alternately maintaining
or abandoning their heritage is signified by the narrator's family
ritualistically breaking candy bars in their Newark alley while
the Patimkins spend thousands for cosmetic nose surgery ("I knew
Mr. Patimkin would never bother to have that stone cut from
his face, and yet, with joy and pride, no doubt, had paid to have
Brenda's diamond removed and dropped down some toilet in
Fifth Avenue Hospital" [p. 28]). The narrator's sensibility is
further expanded through the repertoire of his daily life, alternately resenting the socially grotesque librarians he works with
in Newark (stereotypically defined by their dress and habits) and
then preferring them to the Ivy League snobbery he encounters
among the Patimkins. A rather simple system of signs is his
encouragement to make a final choice: the introduction of a young
black ghetto dweller who is fascinated with the escapist imagery
of Paul Gauguin, and whom the narrator must protect from the

supercilious library staff. In these circumstances it is an automatic association for both narrator and reader: "Short Hills, which I could see now, in my mind's eye, at dusk, rose-colored, like a Gauguin stream" (p. 38). These signs, however, can be and are reversed for the novel's climax. In crisis, Brenda turns to the attic filled with the family's old Newark-days furniture; the narrator encounters Mr. Patimkin in circumstances which show his true nature, among the warehouse stock of his business, Patimkin Kitchen and Bathroom Sinks (located, significantly, in the black section of Newark); and the nebulous ideality of the love affair is concretized (and hence made vulnerable) by the mother's discovery of Brenda's contraceptive device. At this point the entire relationship is called to the court of consciousness, where the hard reality of signs ends the affair.

"What was it inside me," the narrator asks, "that had turned pursuit and clutching into love, and then turned it inside out again?" (p. 135). The question is easily answered, because the drama has been one of clearly recognizable, easily manageable signs. Knowing what to do with them before he or she reads the book, the reader must simply decipher Roth's social objects—first from word to thing, then from thing to its place and meaning in the world. For the contemporaries of 1959, the process is virtually automatic, and even future uncertainties can be resolved with historically explanatory footnotes (the following decade's film of *Goodbye, Columbus* remained current with its own age yet textually true to the novella by substituting birth control pills for 1959's state-of-the-art diaphragm). The quasi-fictive work is as stable or as fluid as the object-world it describes.

As fiction, *Goodbye, Columbus* prescribes an action which takes place out in another field of discourse among familiar signs of middle-class American life. The signs themselves are so common and inclusive (shabby poverty in city ghettos, snobbish affluence in the suburbs) that thorough artistic control of the novella's materials is lost at the moment of reading, when words are loosed from the page and sail out blindly toward their gargantuan targets of bourgeois manners. Once read, the novel is remembered not as an assemblage of words but rather as a collection of images. The reader will recall the picture of a country club dance in Short Hills, New Jersey, with no specific awareness of the language which created it—precisely because the story has taken place in a world of signs, within a theater of memories and associations of country clubs, dances, and social occasions collected all through life. That the thematic development of *Goodbye, Columbus* remains on track is a testament to its author's choice of unambiguous signs over which there can be no expected debate; the novel is indeed turned loose among the readers' world of signs, but their use is so predictable that Roth has taken very little risk. The readers' imagining has already been done for them—by the author.

Determination, however, is not the same achievement as control. And to exercise control in fiction the author must somehow bound his or her text. That such control is still possible while working with signs is shown by Kurt Vonnegut's short piece, "The Hyannis Port Story," which by its choice of a much smaller world of more localized signs makes these objects more apparent as themselves.

Roth and Vonnegut wrote their respective works at approximately the same time (1959, 1963) for the same popular American readership. Each work relies on signs to express its action. But while Roth's system of reference is so broad and self-effacing (in favor of general truths) as to be readable within a fifty-year span of bourgeois culture, Vonnegut's scheme of sign-objects is emphatically specific; indeed, the references of "The Hyannis Port Story" are so coherently particularized that they point almost entirely to themselves. Even at its time of intended publication the story presumed a readership knowledgeable about the fine points of American politics and the political news of the day—for instance, that former President Dwight Eisenhower was never fully accepted by the Republican Right who preferred Senator Robert Taft, that Walter Reuther of the United Auto Workers was an ideological ally of President John Kennedy, and that Adlai Stevenson's ambassadorship to the United Nations was an ironic end to his almost saintly career in defense of American liberalism. As little as a decade later these references have to be explained for the story to work; however, the artificial acts of footnoting or historical research serve to keep the story bounded as a text, for there is no way the signs can run free among a reader's automatic associations. As written, they pertain to an extremely local situation which itself features an unconventional contamination of history with dream, as real-life figures such as Kennedy, Stevenson, and Reuther are mixed in with overtly fictional characters and wildly improbable action more appropriate to fiction than to fact. Hence despite its use of signs, "The Hyannis Port Story" never invites the reader to confuse it with history. The signs are self-apparently fictional and help create a partially bounded text.

"The poetic function [of language] projects the principle of equivalence from the axis of selection into the axis of combination," writes Roman Jakobson,[4] and because the linguistic signs of "The Hyannis Port Story" mean more among themselves than in reference to the outside world, Vonnegut's language can be assumed to be more self-apparent than Roth's. To emphasize the self-contained world of his fiction, Vonnegut chooses a narrator whose speaking voice is the center for everything. "The farthest away from home I ever sold a storm window was in Hyannis Port, Massachusetts, practically in the front yard of President Kennedy's summer home," he begins. All distance is measured from his point of view, encompassing two signs (the homely occupation of selling storm windows, the lofty glamor of the Kennedy family) which by themselves might direct the reader outward into a world of personal associations, but which here in their very unlikeliness of fusion set a boundary within which the reader's interest must play. In terms of national importance (and of the more common perspective which uses signs as references to a shared social world), Vonnegut's point of view is cockeyed;

measuring points should emanate from the presidency, much as the centralized French highway system is plotted from Kilometer Zero in the heart of Paris. But for a uniquely self-contained and self-apparent world of signs—the narrator's, the story's—North Crawford, New Hampshire, is a legitimate standard.

For Vonnegut's narrator, national politics are less important than the hassles of his job, and this deliberate confusion sets the story in motion. A Lion's Club speech (by a young political conservative named Robert Taft Rumfoord) is followed by a bitter argument between the narrator and one of his customers over a leaky bathtub enclosure. The boy's father, however, thinks the fight is about his son's speech and that the narrator is defending the platform of conservative republicanism, and so gratefully orders a full set of combination storms for his Hyannis Port mansion. The action is now under way, with the narrator swept up into a world of signs and symbols to which he could never be expected to relate. It's summer 1963, with the Kennedy family at the height of faddishness, and Hyannis is awash with sightseers and celebrities. In a traffic jam outside town Vonnegut arranges his first confrontation between signs from different worlds (history/fiction, high estate/low estate).

> I was feeling pretty sorry for myself, because I was just an ordinary citizen, and had to get stuck in lines like that. But then I recognized the man in the limousine up ahead of me. It was Adlai Stevenson. He wasn't moving any faster than I was, and his radiator was boiling too.
>
> One place there, we got stuck so long that Mr. Stevenson and I got out and walked around a little. I took the opportunity to ask him how the United Nations were getting along. He told me they were getting along about as well as could be expected. That wasn't anything I didn't already know. (P. 136).

Already, within the story's first two episodes, a structure for dealing with these signs has been established. Whether confronted with the eccentric Commodore Rumfoord in New Hampshire or the stately Adlai Stevenson on the road to Hyannis Port, the narrator imposes his own homely order on these references to a world both fancier and crazier than his own. As the story moves to its center point, the signs of loftiness and absurdity increase in density. In one remarkable paragraph the narrator finds himself in town, driving past such objects as the Presidential Motor Inn, the First Family Waffle Shop, the PT-109 Cocktail Lounge, and—in climactic silliness—a miniature golf course named The New Frontier. Able to handle just half of this, and also needing lunch, he stops at the Waffle Shop but is again stymied by a set of ridiculous signs: the different kinds of waffles are named after members of the Kennedy family and their entourage. "A waffle with strawberries and cream was a *Jackie*," we're told. "A waffle with a scoop of ice cream," quite naturally, "was a *Caroline*." What comes next? Vonnegut's ascending structure of absurdities makes it seem inevitable—"They even had a waffle named *Arthur Schlesinger, Jr.*" But the story's structure has also let the mundane narrator not only make the best of it in such situations but also transform them to his own standard. "I had a thing called a *Teddy*," which he gratefully declines to describe, "and a cup of *Joe*" (pp. 136–37).

From here the story accelerates to its midpoint, as the narrator arrives at the Rumfoord mansion. Down the street, past the presidential compound he drives, closer and closer to the massive Rumfoord home decked out like a medieval castle with its towers and balconies. The last thing he notes, however, is the most improbable (yet, within the story's system of self-apparent signs, most inevitable). "On a second-floor balcony was a huge portrait of Barry Goldwater. It had bicycle reflectors in the pupils of its eyes. Those eyes stared right through the Kennedy gate. There were floodlights all around it, so I could tell it was lit up at night. And the floodlights were rigged with blinkers."

At this point the story breaks; its author provides a line or two of blank space while the narrator settles down to get his bearings. "A man who sells storm windows can never be really sure about what class he belongs to," he tells himself, "especially if he installs the windows, too" (p. 137). So he prepares to keep out of the way, do his job, and hurry back to the sounder world of North Crawford, New Hampshire. But the commodore draws him in once more, this time to a world of political prejudices and comically neurotic behavior. The climax to this second section comes when young Robert Taft Rumfoord is apprehended aboard the presidential yacht *Marlin*, where Adlai Stevenson and Walter Reuther have been conferring. "Stevenson and Reuther?" the commodore blusters, "That's the last time I let my son go swimming without a dagger in his teeth. I hope he was opening the seacocks when beaten insensible by truncheons" (p. 141). In fact, Robert had been using the boat for rendezvous with Sheila Kennedy, the president's fourth cousin. Even more devastating to the commodore is the news that the two are about to be married.

"With Goldwater's floodlights turned off, and with my son engaged to marry a Kennedy," the utterly deflated old man now admits, "what am I but what the man on the sight-seeing boat said I was: A man who sits on this porch, drinking martinis, and letting the old mazooma roll in." His wife reminds him that she agrees with the working world that it's hard to admire a man "who actually doesn't do anything" (p. 144). Of course, there has been an interloper from this other working world all along— the narrator—and his presence helps readjust the order of competing signs: from the dominance of rich, glamorous, and somewhat absurd references which so often threatened to eclipse the homely and mundane to a system which reestablishes the latter as the norm. In this sense "The Hyannis Port Story" and *Goodbye, Columbus* conclude at the same point; the crucial difference is that Vonnegut's story never takes these signs for granted—the normative is a mode sought for and won only after a highly artificial and self-apparent struggle.

Moreover, "The Hyannis Port Story" has not really ended with the commodore's reform, for the self-apparent life of signs needs to be redefined within his new attitude. In a brief coda to the commodore's repentant speech, Vonnegut's narrator introduces the famous personage whose absence has been a matter of growing suspense. In the evening's quiet two cars pull in the driveway, stop beneath the darkened Goldwater sign—"And I heard the voice of the President of the United States coming from the car in front." Will the commodore please light the sign? asks the president; he has Khrushchev's son-in-law along and would like to show it off. Of course, the commodore respectfully replies. "He turned it on," the narrator reports, and "The whole neighborhood was bathed in flashing light." An actual Soviet Communist in Kennedy's camp, the insult of the Goldwater display—are these signs about to lose their self-apparency and fly toward their referential targets in the supposedly real world, angering the commodore and ridiculing the president? Hardly so, because for the president the sign has been self-apparent all along. "And *leave* it on, would you please?" the president adds. "That way I can find my way home" (p. 145).

Whereas in Philip Roth's *Goodbye, Columbus* the social material described is only an instrument of signification for a drama taking place among functional worldly values, for Kurt Vonnegut's "The Hyannis Port Story" the objects described are their own signifier, existing as far as the story's strategy in and for themselves. The refrigerators, neighborhoods, and contraceptive devices of Roth's work were used for what they tell us about the style of life in the world; identical points could have been made with other objects such as washing machines, vacations, and the like. But in "The Hyannis Port Story" the Goldwater sign becomes more of an icon than a functionally representative device. It means nothing other than itself, and within the fiction's circumscribed world can be used for whatever improvised purpose a character wants: as an insult to a neighbor, or as a night-light to guide one's way home. Outside the story it signifies something quite different, but Vonnegut has been careful to make all his indicators point inwards, toward the text at hand.

Vonnegut's self-apparency is accomplished without any of the foregrounding of technique by which certain modes of storytelling show their artificiality of manner. "The Hyannis Port Story" is narrated in precisely the same straightforward way as *Goodbye, Columbus*, and its materials are equally signs. The difference is that Vonnegut's signs, when directed outward toward the real world, would confuse and dissatisfy the reader—hence the author's reputation as "crazy" and "bizarre." The story's compact structure, however, invites a more fruitful association of these signs within their own provisional universe. Their silliness, moreover, draws attention to their patently artificial and self-contained system of reference (First Family Waffle Shop, PT-109 Cocktail Lounge, and so forth). Even a self-conscious narrator telling a story about his own book's composition (the most extreme method of technical foregrounding to be studied in chapter 4) cannot escape the fact that the components of fiction, unlike the notes of music and daubs of paint in abstractly expressive works, are necessarily referential. Words *mean*. For fiction to be truly self-apparent, the author must devise ways of making these references point inward, to the work itself, rather than in a functionally conceptual manner toward the world outside. Having the signs of discourse make better sense among themselves than in reference to the social world is one way to reach this end.

Kurt Vonnegut makes his narrator the source of all measure— a middle-class man whose skeptical glance at the signs and symbols of Hyannis Port reduces them to meaninglessness (that is, in any system other than Hyannis Port's own). Another way is to make the narrator's voice so idiosyncratic and unbelievable beyond its own momentum that the reader's attention is kept firmly within the speaker's own off-beat world of references. Hughes Rudd, one of Vonnegut's contemporaries in age and publishing his early fiction about the same time and in the same magazines as Vonnegut and Roth, is a master of this style. "Miss Euayla Is the Sweetest *Thang!*" is Hughes Rudd's *tour de force* of self-apparent narrative language.[5] The storyteller, Lafond T. Cummingham ("no bigger than a shotgun," as he describes himself), would have the reader believe he has suffered an unfair living crucifixion at the hands of the dull South Texas yokels who have obstructed his courtship of the local belle and heiress, Miss Euayla. His tales are full of reference to the outside world—the "jealous person" up in Fort Worth who stole his guitar case, the radio-station manager who thinks he's a dangerously excitable extrovert—but none of them makes sense the way Lafond would like. Indeed, the story is so full of contradictions, false pieties, and idiotic posturings that one soon decides Lafond is a self-deceiving fool. Unwilling to believe in Lafond's wacky system of signs for what they refer to, the reader takes delight in their self-apparency: how they provide a running source of amusement by signifying nothing so much as their narrator's wackiness. Creating such self-apparency is, of course, an art, and Hughes Rudd is careful that every passing reference to the supposedly lovely Miss Euayla includes notice of her taste for roast beef sandwiches (a caloric intake soon running in the tens of thousands). Again, the signs make better sense (and provide more enjoyment) among themselves than in reference to the world.

A third way of keeping language self-apparent is the collage effect: mixing together various signs which by themselves are properly referential, but when combined in a realistically impossible way draw more attention to themselves. Bernard Malamud's "The Jewbird"[6] takes a familiar scene, almost narcotic in its familiarity of referential associations, and collages in one unlikely element—a talking bird as the stand-in for a predictably uncomfortable relative living with a younger family—which throws the entire narrative into self-apparency. Donald Barthelme's "Porcupines at the University"[7] takes the equally tired situation of student protest and minority discrimination on a typical sixties campus and revitalizes it by replacing the disaffected students with porcupines. For Barthelme collage is more of a compositional technique than figurative device, emphasizing the presence of the artifact rather than its objects of depiction. It is, he told a *New York Times* interviewer, "the central principle of all art in the twentieth century in all media,"[8] adding in a subsequent discussion that the point of collage is that unlike things are stuck together to make, in the best case, a new reality. This new reality, in the best case, may be or imply a comment on the other reality from which it came, and may also be much else. It's an *itself*, if it's successful: Harold Rosenberg's "anxious object," which does not know whether it's a work of art or a pile of junk.[9]

The secret to making such an integral object is to keep each constituent element self-apparent, so that its reference value is blunted in favor of a more effective construct of self-meaning. In "Porcupines at the University" three perfectly normal sign-systems from the real world—that of college administrators, cowboys, and porcupines—are thrown together in a totally ludicrous mélange. Their mutual improbability is reinforced throughout the story as they steadfastly act in character—the dean speaks in blank verse while his wife puzzles whether the unwanted porcupines could "enroll in Alternate Lifestyles"; the porcupine wranglers banter phrases among themselves such as "What say potner?" "How about vamoosing?" and "I guess we better parley"; and the porcupines behave simply like porcupines. Even the scenery is stock material from a Marlboro cigarette commercial, perfect in every detail except for the presence of those madly impossible animals.

> Meanwhile the porcupine wrangler was wrangling the porcupines across the dusty and overbuilt West.
> Dust clouds. Yips. The lowing of porcupines.
> "Git along theah li'l porcupines."

In other stories, such as "Paraguay" and "Bone Bubbles," Barthelme uses words themselves as materials for his collage, as he explained to anthologist Rust Hills:

> Mixing bits of this and that from various areas of life to make something that did not exist before is an oddly hopeful endeavor. The sentence "Electrolytic jelly exhibiting a capture ratio far in excess of standard is used to fix animals in place" made me very happy—perhaps in excess of its merit. But there is in the world such a thing as electrolytic jelly; the "capture ratio" comes from the jargon of sound technology; and the animals themselves are a salad

of the real and the invented. The flat, almost "dead" tone paradoxically makes possible an almost-lyricism.[10]

Within the syntax of sound-technology the words "capture ratio" might not draw attention to themselves, for they would be in the process of signifying something about audio equipment; but in a sentence where no rational reference is possible, they can be appreciated for themselves. In a fiction symposium Barthelme made the point again.

> One of the funny things about experimentalism in regard to language is that most of it has not been done yet. Take *mothball* and *vagina* and put them together and see if they mean anything together; maybe you're not happy with the combination and you throw that on the floor and pick up the next two and so on. There's a lot of basic research which hasn't been done because of the enormous resources of the language and the enormous number of resonances from the past which have precluded this way of investigating language.[11]

Barthelme is right: because they are handled mostly in terms of their significations, words are rarely used for their own properties—at least not by fictionists, whose uncertainty and insecurity of form have given them a built-in imperative for relating to the world. The collage method of treating words as material is one strategy; another is to let the words combine to form references, but in a deliberately unlikely way. Of this technique Richard Brautigan is the master. His novel *Trout Fishing in America*[12] has little plot, character, or action, and its theme consists in stretching metaphors to incredible lengths between tenor and vehicle. California's sylvan Big Sur area, for example, is introduced as a "thousand-year-old flophouse for mountain lions and lilacs"; a person's birthmark "looked just like an old car parked on his head"; an untended graveyard is described as "for the poor and it had no trees and the grass turned a flat-tire brown in the summer and stayed that way until the rain, like a mechanic, began in the late autumn" (and when the fall rains come, they do their work "like a sleepy short-order cook cracking eggs over

a grill next to a railroad station" [pp. 20–21]). Such verbal ac-
robatics transcend the referential and redirect interest toward
the making of metaphors on the page, where the attention is
less toward the conceptualization of either the thing itself or to
what it's compared, and more to the distance between them, the
arena of the writer's art.

Realistic signs used unrealistically frustrate a referential reading and send the reader back to the text to find out what has
gone wrong. Once there, curiosity involves itself in the pathology of deconceptualized language to the point where such language becomes its own reason for being, much as a super-sleuth
detective can become so caught up in the process of ratiocination
that the investigation is forgotten or at least made far less interesting. Reference is part of the process, but only because words
are congenitally conceptual. By blocking what the reader wants
to do with words and making this disruption a more satisfying
process to follow, the self-apparent fictionist has taken the genre's
weakest point and made it a tactical strength.

Robert Coover has built a canon of works dedicated to the
independence language can achieve within a work of fiction. His
first novel, *The Origin of the Brunists*,[13] was written as an exercise
in formal realism, even though its theme concerns the transformative power of a vatic cult over a common American town. His
second novel, *The Universal Baseball Association, J. Henry Waugh,
Prop.*,[14] incorporates such transformations within its own narrative structure: a card-table baseball game slowly becomes its
own reality as the narrative center shifts from the player above
to the players on the field. *The Public Burning*[15] uses a similar
approach to the reality/fantasy axis to trick not just the characters but the reader as well. In this third novel curious yet historically true materials from American politics of the early 1950s
are combined with utterly fatuous details, a mixture so homog-
enous that the reader must use encyclopediae and almanacs to
sort out fact from invention, as in the following scene of Julius
and Ethel Rosenberg's execution.

A band is hired to play "One Fine Day" from *Madame Butterfly*, "The Anniversary Waltz," and the theme from *High Noon*, said to be a particular favorite these days of President Eisenhower, who is himself just back from a week of moralizing and whoopee in the Badlands and Oyster Bay. Gene Autry visits the President and is invited to sing "Tumblin' Tumbleweeds" and "Twilight on the Trail" at the executions; the National Poet Laureate TIME is asked to read a commemorative poem; Ethel Rosenberg's kid brother David Greenglass ("little Doovey," she called him), the confessed traitor whose evidence has almost singlehandedly convicted Ethel and her husband and sent them to the chair, is invited to retell his heart-warming story for the edification of the gathered faithful and to remind Julius for the last time that he still owes him a thousand bucks; and from East Berlin comes the Red flag, torn down by rioting workers from the Brandenburg Gate, to be cut and sewn into a suit of longjohns for Julius to wear during his electrocution. This uprising in Berlin, just one day before the intended ceremonial extinction of the Rosenbergs, is Uncle Sam's crowning touch to over two years of untiring stagecraft, prayer, and arm-to-arm brawls with the Phantom's ubiquitous agents. As TIME say in his famous lyric, "Rebellion in the Rain":

barehanded they gathered in the grey
morning rain—masons in white
carpenters in black day laborers
and factory hands in hobnailed
   boots and raveled suits
in mumbling columns that suggested
disconnected centipede legs groping
for a body they streamed from all
directions toward the center where
   the communist proconsuls rule . . . [16]

The words from *Time* are cited verbatim; Coover's only change is to break them into lines of verse, which transforms the way they are read. The references to Dwight Eisenhower, Gene Autry, and David Greenglass are all accurate—only their combination is false. The Rosenberg matter, the East German revolt, the anti-Communist purges of Senator Joseph McCarthy—all are part of the same historical circumstance, and Coover's sole license has been in a certain foreshortening of events; no one would deny that in the general character of the age they were interconnected. But such appreciation demands a distancing from the objects of reference and a refocused attention on the verbal signs themselves, for only appreciated in their constructive zaniness (who ever could have concocted a fiction as goofy as 1953's reality, we ask ourselves) can the paragraph be understood. So reordered, the predictable significations of a novel like *Goodbye, Columbus* are made to perform a directly opposite function: not for what they mean, but for what they are in themselves.

Coover's story "The Babysitter"[17] combines many strategies for self-apparency: the making of a world those temporal and spatial dimensions are unique to itself, the deliberate confusion of alternate realms of fact and fantasy, and an organizational structure more often cued to words themselves than anything else. In each case conventional expectations are violated; the transparency of technique which directs the reader's attention to the outside world is by the breaking of convention made opaque, so that it obstructs the referential role of fiction and substitutes a self-contained world of story. The language is still conceptual, as it has been in all of these examples, but the conceptualization is now focused on the story's own structure rather than its message about the world.

The story's context begins with a world of significations as commonly social as Roth's *Goodbye, Columbus*. A teenage babysitter is coming to watch the Tucker's children while the parents have a night out. Yet within the first sentence the presumed reality begins to deconstruct. "She arrives at 7:40, ten minutes late, but the children, Jimmy and Bitsy, are still eating supper, and their parents are not ready to go yet." Elsewhere in the house discreet universes vie for attention ("From other rooms come the sounds of a baby screaming, water running, a television musical . . . "). When Mrs. Tucker appears, her first words confirm that she's been living in her own world of time. "'Harry!' she calls. 'The babysitter's here already!'" (p. 206).

Mr. Tucker inhabits his own distinct spatial world—down

the hall in the bathroom, but also musing lustfully about the sexy young babysitter; his thoughts are appropriately given their own block paragraph. Also set off by itself is a section describing Jack, the babysitter's boyfriend, wrapped up in his own sexual thoughts. The separation of these worlds is reinforced by a corresponding structure in the real world of reference—Mr. Tucker is down the hall, Jack is on the other side of town. But even face to face, within the kitchen, competing worlds collide: to the babysitter's cheery "Hi, what's for supper?" the child Jimmy replies, "I don't have to go to bed until nine" (p. 207).

Such deliberate ruptures of the usual syntax of signification divides Coover's references into their constitutive parts; Jimmy, the babysitter, even Mr. and Mrs. Tucker are seen independently from the central action, which is itself threatening not to coalesce. It is such coherency as lacking here which gathers up the materials of narrative and impels them outward toward the corresponding world of reference. Once begun, this process is almost automatic, and the story begins to tell itself in the reader's mind. "The Babysitter," however, disrupts this mode. From paragraph to paragraph the reader at first does not know what to expect, except the unexpected. But neither is the structure pure chaos. Sections hang together by virtue of associated gestures and in several cases by an identity of words alone which the reader soon comes to appreciate. One paragraph features Mr. Tucker's musings on the nubile babysitter and his own romantic past; meanwhile, as the reader learns in the next section, his wife has been regretting the death of just such romantic times ("He loves her. She loves him. And then the babies come. And dirty diapers and one goddamn meal after another. Dishes. Noise. Clutter. And fat."). In the first section he's noticed her readjusting her garter; now, within her own narrative, she's thinking how her girdle hurts; and in the next paragraph, set back at the house, the kids are struggling to pull down the babysitter's skirt (p. 209). The associations are there, but on a level beyond that of simple cumulative, narrative signification. The reader learns to think in terms of the materials themselves, and of their association not in terms of pantomimic continuity (which effaces the language) but rather in terms of irony, burlesque, or even vulgar humor—all of which demand an awareness of the words themselves. Rather than depending upon a narrative sense of illusion, Coover presents a fiction whose effects are generated by self-consciously structural devices, and with which the reader is invited to play.

Bitsy urinates in the bathtub; Mr. Tucker mixes a bourbon and water. Jack plays a sexually suggestive game of pinball; his friend Mark imagines using the same moves on the babysitter. The materials of each independent scene invite associations independent of the actual narrative line, but indicative of a higher level of *making* which the author has asked the reader to complete. As with cinematic montage, the audience must supply something not physically present within the simple elements of text; but this additional information is not producible without an attention to the existing elements *as materials*.

Nowhere in "The Babysitter" may the reader wander out into the common world of references and be comfortable very long, for each caesural break between paragraph sections reminds one that there is no common world to be shared. In one section Mr. Tucker has imagined how the babysitter and her boyfriend will be deep into heavy sex by mid-evening, and so at what he conceives to be just the right moment finds a pretext to come home. "Hey! What's going on here?" he shouts, stumbling in like an actor off-cue, for in this the babysitter's paragraph there's no sex at all, just popcorn and TV (p. 229). Because there is no commonly shared world to which these signs may point, the reader is kept within the story's own artificial bounds. The language is still referential, but now the references are working on the page rather than in the world.

"The Babysitter" is not, strictly speaking, a work of pure language, since even within its bounded texts signs are asked to work as signs rather than as words. For the matters of one's own memories, however, the question stays open: within the bounded text of personal recall, do we remember signs themselves or the words which form them? And when story takes the form of memory, are we given self-apparent words? Ronald Sukenick's "Momentum,"[18] a demonstration even more extreme than Coover's story, makes no apologies for form, because its existence is justified by its act of composition—the hurried dictation of memories from a just-concluded trip, a time when "everything came together" and which the author wants to capture before it's lost. An unedited transcription of the hour's tape fills the right-hand column of each page; on the left are editorial comments added later. There are no dissimulating strategies such as Richardson's packet of letters or Sterne's "told" story—"Momentum" is its own reality, the narrative not of a two-day trip to Ithaca but rather of a speaker sitting in his room, talking to a tape recorder, and later adding notes to his text. Hence when Ithaca, New York, itself is named, the author is referring not to the city in upstate New York but rather to an element in his memory, for it is memory and not event being here described.

"Momentum," then, is a story about itself. Its substance is the onward rush of language as it skips through memory in search of the things which impel its forward flow. If the memory deals in language rather than in signs, if it is the word itself which is recalled rather than the cumbersome worldly object or event, then "Momentum" is self-apparent fiction. "okay here we go i don't want to whisper this i want to hear my natural speaking voice the way it really sounds also i can see myself here in a full-length mirror as i speak," the story begins, self-apparent in circumstance and discarding even the routine conventions of punctuation which we use to minimally structure the written word. Soon grammar and syntax vanish as well, with run-on sentences inviting the reader to stumble forward with the text, in synch with the narrator's rush to get it all said. The elements of recall are similarly sketchy: a crazy lady on the bus trip north who insists we all need more oxygen, random views of the Cor-

nell campus which themselves bring back memories from under-
graduate days ten years before, lovely coeds (everywhere), the
adventure of buying an old car, renting an apartment, going to
a party, picking up a young woman. Few of them are worthy as
signs in themselves, for none tells a story, invites associations,
or counsels judgments like the materials of *Goodbye, Columbus*.
In "Momentum" these objects exist only in memory (a marginal
note says "Real means locating the present in terms of the past
locating the self in terms of the present. Wordsworth, Proust,"
p. 13), and the real action is having things fall in place within
the narrator's mind. An experience larger than the parts so named
is being articulated in his memory. Within the experience of
signs, the event is almost laughable ("i had found an apartment
i had found a car and now i'd found finally a coed whose ass i not
only admired walking across campus but which i could also
squeeze," p. 32), but the real point has been "past and present
each defining each finally finding balance" (p. 33), making past
and present integral to one's constant self: "unity of experience
= reality of self" (p. 38). The narrator has opened up a reality
larger than he'd known before, simply because he's now in touch
with more of himself. Whatever signs have been used point inward to his own constructing consciousness. Words have been
used as words, to articulate the patterns they've made in his own
mind.

By discarding every device from punctuation to structured
narrative, Ronald Sukenick's "Momentum" manages to use words
as integers of fiction itself. Yet "Momentum" is definitely fiction
stripped bare, leaving just the experience of assembling words
in a manner which articulates a personal view. It is the ultimate
contraction of fiction from the cumbersome strategies of Richardson, Sterne, and Fielding.

As fiction expands again from this essence, self-effacement vies
again with self-apparency in language. Chapter 3 will consider
to what extent the word-salad of James Joyce and the automatic
writing of Gertrude Stein are self-apparent. Their universe is

larger than Sukenick's, but how much of it is substructured in myth or psychology? Does *Ulysses* mean itself in terms of language, or does it depend even in part upon Homeric legend for its larger sense? Closer to the present, are the cutups of William Burroughs functional as fiction, or is their existence justified only by the negatively mechanical nature of their origin? Alain Robbe-Grillet's *nouveau roman* is faithful to the surface description of phenomenology, but to what extent has Jacques Derrida's deconstruction of "presence" revealed a logocentric myth in this style of fiction? Finally, when Sukenick's own strategy of writing about his own work's composition is expanded and developed to novel length, is there not a risk that the old Aristotelian convention which has bogged fiction's legitimacy from the start might creep back in, and that the self-reflective novel becomes nothing more than the imitation of an imitation of an action? The antidote to such mimetic poison is an approach to fiction which demands no excuse for language other than its own being: a short story or novel whose every device points the signifying power of words back inward toward the text itself.

chapter 3   STRATEGIES AGAINST
EFFACEMENT

From James Joyce and Gertrude Stein through Samuel Beckett and William S. Burroughs, fiction in English has sought a way beyond the effacement of language. In French literature, a similar tradition stretches from Marcel Proust through Alain Robbe-Grillet to the novelists within the *Tel Quel* group. Among American contemporaries, a number of writers such as Ronald Sukenick, Steve Katz, and Gilbert Sorrentino distinguished themselves in the late 1960s and seventies by experiments with novels alleged to be the stories of their own composition: the author and narrator were one, the novel's central character was the person writing it and the book's action was simply the process of its own composition.

In most cases, however, these strategies stop short of true self-apparency. Joyce grounds his work in psychology and myth, and *Ulysses* can be discussed in such terms without sacrificing an unfair amount of its substance as a novel. As William York Tindall says, "The pattern of Bloom's action is that of almost all men's daily lives: leaving home in the morning, Bloom comes back at night. His day is a journey." Homer's *Odyssey* is one form for such action, but it can also be expressed within the success story model used by Horatio Alger—in each case something is being written *about*, and that external form provides the work's pattern. There is judgment operating here as well. "Clearly," Tindall suggests, "the theme of *Ulysses*, implied by the quest and determined by the characters, is moral."[1] By appeal to or even in parallel with these other systems, *Ulysses* sends the reader beyond the experience of Joyce's writing for the truth of its subjects. *Finnegans Wake* in turn recalls as model *The Book of Kells*, as if even pure improvisation needs an analog before it can exist as fiction. Moreover, the *Wake's* division into four parts evokes a grounding in the four ages of human culture: divine, heroic, human, and regenerative. The language games are most attractive for their psychological patterns; little in Joyce is not grounded elsewhere. The achievement of modernism is noteworthy, and in Joyce's hands the novel underwent great transformation. But his project, as was modernism's in general, was to find how culture could continue without the confident assumptions of nineteenth-century science and philosophy to support it. Linguistic self-apparency was not at issue, and therefore it should not be surprising that Joyce's novels retain a strong element of effacement before the actions of their story.

Grounding one's text in a realm beyond language destroys self-apparency. But so does the foregrounding of language itself, for this latter technique is simply an inversion of the former. Richard Kostelanetz has described Gertrude Stein's effort to build a complex literary style without using the customary "arsenal of devices that authors had traditionally used to enhance their prose." One of Stein's achievements was to employ "the shifting of syntax, so that parts of a sentence appear in unusual places."[2] Another was repetition, varying the relationships words have according to their changing frames. Such writing is part of the "defamiliarization" the Russian Formalists encouraged as a way of highlighting the language of one's texts. Yet Victor Shklovsky's description of how such defamiliarization works belies its representational origins. Proofreading one's own manuscript is always difficult, he argues, because our familiarity with its language encourages us to pass directly into the world it represents, and as a result we can be blind to the most obvious typographical errors. In such circumstances we are not reading words, we are recognizing a message. By foregrounding the mechanics of one's literary art (using self-conscious metaphors, emphasizing one's artifice of construction) or by defamiliarizing one's language (as in Stein's example), the writer draws attention to the words on the page. Yet when all is done, the messages are still there, whether or not the techniques are foregrounded and the language defamiliarized. At best the Formalists' techniques temporarily redirect the reader, by the most mechanical of means, and in subsequent encounters leave the danger of falling victim again to familiarity. Shklovsky assumes that our own manuscript is a representational work in the first place; his is merely a strategy to make the artifice of representation more clear.

Strategies against effacement are also evident in the works of William S. Burroughs. Not one of his novels from *Naked Lunch* (1959) through *Nova Express* (1965) can be read without notice of its violent, repulsive language. Burroughs seizes upon words one usually shies away from and holds each before the eye; his scenes are so disturbing that it is no welcome process to pass through language to event, and so attention is riveted all the more on those horrific words themselves. Yet it is the signified event which has made these words so shocking in the first place, and even though the language which connotes them has since taken on its own life (and can indeed be routinely applied to other systems of reference, as in the overuse of sexual and scatological diction), it is the nature of what these words simply signify and the actions they represent that draw attention. Burroughs' fiction, then, still depends upon a world of signifieds for its signifiers to work as they do.

When critics describe Burroughs as a satirist and he describes himself as a psychic explorer, the grounding of his novels becomes even more evident. His subject matter vitalizes language, not the other way around, and his writing technique is drawn from the heroin addict's hypersensitized perception.

> During withdrawal the addict is acutely aware of his surroundings. Sense impressions are sharpened to the point of hallucination. Familiar objects seem to stir with a writhing furtive life. The addict is subject to a barrage of sensations external and visceral. He may experience flashes of beauty and nostalgia, but the overall impression is extremely painful—(Possibly his sensations are painful because of their intensity. A pleasurable sensation may become intolerable after a certain intensity is reached.)[3]

The "naked lunch" itself is that moment of awareness, when the food is poised at the fork's end, of how cannibalistic life really is. Again, the mode of perception has been through drugs (a mechanical alteration of reality), and Burroughs introduces the volume with a "Deposition: Testimony Concerning a Sickness" which is itself preceded by obscenity trial transcripts and the United States Supreme Court's judgment that the book has "redeeming social importance"—the ultimate witness, here made part of the novel itself, that *Naked Lunch* is a work grounded in the worldly real.

Burroughs' subsequent technique of using cut-ups and fold-ins by which words are transcribed outside of their customary syntactic order also brings a certain attention to language, though he has been careful to indicate that its ultimate goal lies elsewhere. The act of reading, Burroughs insists, is on the wane. "To compete with television and photo magazines writers will have to develop more precise techniques producing the same effect on the reader as a lurid action photo." Cut-ups are encouraged by the same challenge that prompts self-apparency of language, that "the painter can touch and handle his medium and the writer cannot."[4] Randomly cutting up and folding in words does give them a materiality apart from their originally intended references, but the comparison to an action photo still invites a pass-through to connotation. At best those connotations are now more artificial and less like something already existing in the world; collages are in this case made out of words themselves rather than word-images (such as Donald Barthelme's porcupines, cowboys, and deans discussed in chapter 2). But language is not Burroughs' object. His most thorough book of cut-ups, *The Third Mind*, is inaugurated with an interview excerpt claiming that "silence is . . . the *most* desirable state." And silence is an experience beyond words.

> In one sense a special use of words and pictures can conduce silence. The scrapbooks and time travel [roots of the cut-up method] are exercises to expand consciousness, to teach me to think in association blocks rather than words. I've recently spent a little time studying hieroglyph systems, both the Egyptian and the Mayan. A whole block of associations—boonf!—like that! Words—at least the way we use them—can stand in the way of what I call nonbody experience. It's true we thought about leaving the body behind.[5]

Reality is still behind the remnant of Burroughs' language which does speak. "The Burroughs machine, systematic and repetitive, simultaneously disconnecting and reconnecting—it disconnects the concept of reality that has been imposed on us and then plugs normally dissociated zones into the same sector," says Gérard-Georges Lemaire in another prefatory section to *The Third Mind*. The author's silence comes when the machine-produced text "eventually escapes from the control of its manipulator" (p. 17). At this point Burroughs' most radical innovation closes the circle with Philip Roth's conservativism, for the cut-up apparatus and *Goodbye, Columbus*'s world of socially accepted signs are equally machines which manufacture meaning. In each case the writer surrenders control as the words efface before their meanings, whether those meanings are produced by a bourgeois system of manners and morals or a mechanical scheme for the cutting and reassemblage of sentences.

The French tradition is equally indebted to the system of signification. Proust's *A la recherche du temps perdu* is the imitation of an imitation of an action, thoroughly Aristotelian in its dependence upon a signified reality. As Steven G. Kellman describes it, "the self-begetting novel . . . projects the illusion of art creating itself";

> This device of a narrative which is in effect a record of its own genesis is a happy fusion of form and content. We are at once confronted with both process and product, quest and goal, parent and child. Proust's *A la recherche du temps perdu* is a history of Marcel's tortuous search for a vocation; at the same time, the very existence of the book itself constitutes objective evidence of Marcel's eventual choice of a literary calling. The nascent fiction gives life to the aging Marcel, who is in turn about to create it. Galatea and Pygmalion embrace.[6]

The form is circular, but the crucial point touched by the circle is representation of an action. Proust's work is paradigm for a style of fiction which will climax in Samuel Beckett's novels as parody. "The project of the self-begetting novel is to create a structure within which its main character and his fiction come to life," Kellman shows (p. 7), but what he is most basically proving is that the self-begetting novel is one more form of representative fiction. It is self-expressive only to the extent that "the hero forges his identity as a novelist and through a novel" (p. 8), an activity quite vulnerable to parody and satire as writers become suspicious of their work. By Beckett's day writing fiction is decried as a cruel lie which prolongs the agony of self. "Each Beckett narrator prolongs his existence and that of the work in which he appears in the very act of assailing both" (p. 11), Kellman concludes, but the ultimate point is that fiction has sought again a real-life existence for itself—here, in its final degradation, as an object of ridicule and scorn by the person who makes it.

The *nouveau roman* or French New Novel is, among other things, an attempt to move beyond parody into writing (and reading) as pure activities, innocent of the judgments Beckett's fiction makes. Surrounded by a great library of theory, including Alain Robbe-Grillet's *Pour un nouveau roman* (1963), Philippe Sollers' *Logiques*

(1968), and the works of Roland Barthes (from his early essays and the book *Le Degré zéro de l'écriture* in 1953 to the posthumous publications following his death in 1980), the *nouveau roman* is as much a critique of earlier forms of fiction as it is a positive contribution on its own.

Barthes describes an "episteomological break" at the end of the nineteenth century, marked by the texts of Lautréamont, Mallarmé, Roussel, Joyce, and Artaud and supported by Gaston Bachelard's work in the philosophy of science, which alters the conditions of reading and writing alike. The novel, as we have seen in chapter 2, was born into a world secure in its own reality and insistent that this new literary form share the same ground-ing—hence the acceptable "excuse" for fiction as a packet of let-ters, manuscript found in a bottle, narrated tale, or the like. For French literature the conventional novel's triumph comes with Balzac, who described himself as "a secretary to Society" and whose language of fiction is identical with the social world it signifies. Control of such work thus leaves the author's hand and is projected out into historical existence; the degree of risk de-pends upon how stable and predictable that world of values is. As Barthes indicates:

> History, then, confronts the writer with a necessary option between several moral attitudes connected with languages; it forces him to signify Literature in terms of possibilities outside his control. We shall see, for example, that the ideological unity of the bourgeoisie gave rise to a single mode of writing, and that in the bourgeois periods (classical and romantic), literary form could not be divided because conscious consciousness was not.[7]

Universal confidence in this system of reference minimizes the risk. Yet this very confidence also insures the transparency of language. When the epistemological break occurs, therefore, confidence in the signified fades and awareness of signifier (lit-erary form) becomes possible.

As soon as the writer ceased to be a witness to the universal, to become the incarnation of a tragic awareness (around 1850), his first gesture was to choose the commitment of his form, either by adopting or rejecting the writer of his past. Classical writing therefore disintegrated, and the whole of Literature, from Flaubert to the present day, became the problematics of language.

This was precisely the time when Literature (the word having come into being shortly before) was finally established as an object. Classical art could have no sense of being a language, for it *was* language, in other words it was transparent, it flowed and left no deposit, it brought ideally together a universal Spirit and a decorative sign without substance or responsibility; it was a language "closed" by social and not natural bounds. It is a well-known fact that towards the end of the eighteenth century this transparency becomes clouded; literary form develops a second-order power independent of its economy and euphemistic charm; it fascinates the reader, it strikes him as exotic, it enthralls him, it acquires a weight. Literature is no longer felt as a socially privileged mode of transportation, but as a language having body and hidden depths, existing both as dream and menace. (P. 3)

It is supposedly the *nouveau roman* which is tailored in this latter mode. "The act of reading has become more difficult," Alain Robbe-Grillet agrees, because "modern fiction demands from the reader a participation that is akin to creation." With each reading, the reader "must organize orders and at the same time perceive breaks with the very orders he himself is introducing." Obviously, this activity cannot take place within the realm of the signified; as an act shared by author and audience it must happen within language itself. "This movement which creates order within the apparent disorder of a work of fiction *is* the act of reading."[8]

Yet a certain signified "reality" does remain in the fiction written by Robbe-Grillet and described by Barthes. What was formerly *depicted* is now "deconstructed" and seen as a mode of production. But a signified reality is there, just as much as a theatrical production still takes place on stage even while those with a technical interest may be watching what happens in the wings. There has been a shift in emphasis, and certainly a suspension of the suspension of disbelief. Reality itself is no longer described, but the experience of that reality (in epistemological terms) is reactivated in reading—reality is still there as fiction's necessary element, albeit now handled in a more analytical way. For Robbe-Grillet's kind of novel, reality has simply changed place, from the cinemascope theatre of projected illusions to "the screen of the mind of the central perceiving character, locus of undifferentiated projection of images of perception and imagination, reality and fantasy."[9] These images are to be presented free from metaphor, especially those anthropomorphic suggestions which in their projection of human qualities smother the object and prevent us from seeing what's actually there. "Purified of the human thickness of metaphor," as Stephen Heath puts it, "language can be returned to an immediate instrumentality" (p. 69). Hence the geometrical descriptions of Alain Robbe-Grillet, former agronomic engineer. No metaphor is innocent, he insists; each one clouds the object in attributes it does not possess; reality is falsified. His own method is more precisely empirical.

> To record the distance between the object and myself, and the distances of the object itself (its *exterior distances*, i.e., its measurements), and the distances of objects among themselves, and to insist further on the fact that these are *only distances* (and not divisions), this comes down to establishing that things are here and that they are nothing but things, each limited to itself. The problem is no longer to choose between a happy correspondence and a painful solidarity. There is henceforth a rejection of all complicity.[10]

Barthes complains the same way about how "man never confronts the object, which remains dutifully subjugated to him by precisely what it is assigned to provide."[11] Such practice, he insists, makes for a great loss. "Behold then a real transformation of the object," Barthes laments, "which no longer has an essence but takes refuge entirely within its attributes. A more complete subservience of things is unimaginable" (p. 6). Such a state recalls the world before 1850, when universal confidence in what things meant allowed a literature of exact representation. "A substantive world of man, an adjectival world of things: such is the order of a creation dedicated to contentment" (p. 10). Balzac's novel shares the same smug security as the commercial city of Amsterdam, Barthes' own metaphor within this essay. The only thing wrong with such circumstance is its utter fraudulence for what we know of the world today.

"What Robbe-Grillet seeks to destroy is therefore the adjective," Barthes concludes (in a companion essay of 1954, "Objective Literature"). "Qualification is never, in his writing, anything but spatial, situational, in no case analogical" (p. 17). But what are Robbe-Grillet's motives for this style of writing? To deal with the real object as a thing in itself, and so remain philosophically current with his time. Were these not the identical goals of eighteenth- and nineteenth-century bourgeois fiction? Although a change of manner in writing helps Robbe-Grillet achieve his purpose, fiction still maintains its essential grounding in the signified world; all that has been accomplished is a certain purifying of the sign-making process. The author's later embrace of film confirms this reality-based aesthetic. "This is precisely what makes the cinema an art," he claims in his Introduction to the film script of *Last Year at Marienbad*. "It creates a reality with forms. It is in its form that we must look for its true content."[12] And the forms of cinema, of course, are moving pictures of the object, technology's most fruitful attempt to capture the living thing in itself. The author's later novels transform this technique back into fiction, but at the expense of needing a sociological form. *Project for a Revolution in New York*, for example, plays with a series of signifiers in shifting contexts, but determining their play is the reader's awareness of the pop-pornographical underworld of New York, which is experienced voyeuristically. Robbe-Grillet's novel, therefore, does not thrive on the absence of a transcendental signified which sets its signs loose in play, for they are all tied closely to New York's sociological system.

The world of things is realized in language, Edmund Husserl believed, and it is to capture these elusive objects that the New

Novelists have turned to language, and not the other way around. Transparency of language is discarded not because it ignores the transparency of words, but because it fails to capture the signified object. Throughout *Pour un nouveau roman* Robbe-Grillet emphasizes the thing in the world. A "passion to describe" it, he insists, has dominated the writers from Flaubert to Kafka who follow Barthes' epistemological break (p. 14). It is the fault of language, he claims, that debates rage as to whether the world is significant or absurd; "It *is*, quite simply" (p. 19). "Let it be first of all by their *presence* that objects and gestures establish themselves," he argues (p. 21), and proposes a new literature based around it. "Since it is chiefly in its presence that the world's reality resides, our task is now to create a literature which takes that presence into account" (p. 23). The activities of literature, as might be expected, are directed entirely toward the object: "measuring, locating, limiting, defining" (p. 24). Although these acts of language might be more trustworthy (in an empirical sense) than a literature fogged over with subjective values, Robbe-Grillet's *nouveau roman* would seem to have taken a different course toward "objectivity" than that suggested by Barthes' epistemological split, the aftermath of which was to emphasize the charming, enthralling, and exotic. For Robbe-Grillet, writing becomes a thing in itself only when it matches up scientifically with the described object.

Presence—the word pops up again and again in *Pour un nouveau roman*. Conventional literature lacks it; the New Novel enshrines it. As a reason for being, it insures the ultimate transparency of language even as it dehumanizes language itself, for it serves the identity of signified objects within the act of signification—within the writing process. What was formerly the domain of human prejudice becomes in Robbe-Grillet's hands the calculated shape of objectivity alone. Such a development for fiction would indeed be innovative except for the fact that its premise belies the same humanistic artificiality which Robbe-Grillet claims to erase. Husserl's axiom that the world of things is realized in language anchors Robbe-Grillet's own aesthetic, which supposedly counters four centuries of humanistic projection. That very presence, however, has been shown to be the metaphysical cornerstone of these same cultures—a fraudulent supposition which by Robbe-Grillet's own rules can be completely discredited. "The living present, a concept that cannot be broken down into a subject and attribute," writes Jacques Derrida in his critique of Husserl's theory of signs, "is thus the conceptual foundation of phenomenology as metaphysics."[13] But considering just what language is, Derrida believes, yields a different conclusion and so upsets traditional metaphysics. Saussure's great contribution was showing that language consists of a series of relations which themselves constitute a system (*la langue*) which informs the specifics of day-to-day speech (*la parole*). As Jonathan Culler has explained, the utterances of speech are like the individual plays in a football game. "The actions are meaningful only with respect to a set of institutional conventions."[14] Is there indeed any *presence* (of the signified object, of purposeful identity, of meaning) within *la parole* itself? Derrida would say no. If all meaning and identity derive from the contrasting relationships ordered by a system, then in language there are only differences and no positive terms in themselves.

Derrida's critique begins with language but encompasses all modern metaphysics which, he argues, has been based on logic (the abstract internal relationship) rather than rhetoric (which Peirce, Royce, Wittgenstein, and Austin have employed as an operational procedure). Logical space founds itself on the presence of simple and eternal objects; but if the world of things is realized in language (Husserl) and language itself is simply a system of relationships preceding any real content (Saussure), the "realization" which does happen within language is something other than logical. Signification, Derrida insists, begins only with a movement away from presence, for all meaning is in the play of differences. Yet because we stand within language, we can never hope to possess (as would Robbe-Grillet) an unpolluted sense of those things in themselves.

The *nouveau roman*, then, does just the opposite of what it intends. Robbe-Grillet's aesthetic is based on the novelist using language to make the world's objects present to himself; every facet of his writing is applied to the capturing of that object in its material qualities, free of imposed humanisms which would obscure it. This aesthetic, however, is based on the metaphysics of presence which Derrida discredits. Speech gives the illusion that the signified is present to the speaker, in his or her mind, at the moment of utterance. Writing reminds us of the separation between element and meaning, and of how the only sense we make is within the play of difference. To base one's work on presence is therefore to project the same humanizing illusions which Robbe-Grillet sought to expel from his writing. "To deconstruct logocentrism" as Derrida does, says Jonathan Culler, "is to show that what was taken to be the truth of the world or the ground of an enquiry is in fact a construct that has been imposed and which is contradicted by certain results of the enquiry it founds." [15] Attempts to deny the primacy of writing and to treat it as form of speech (and hence rely on presence) make it "a parasitic form, the representation of a representation" (p. 139) and even farther from the self-apparency we seek in fiction.

What do we find in language, if not the trace of signifieds themselves? Signs in language share a strange being, admits Gayatri Chakravorty Spivak in the translator's preface to Derrida's *Of Grammatology*: "half of it is always 'not there' and the other half always 'not that.' The structure of the sign is determined by the trace or track of that other which is forever absent." [16] The notion of *trace* not only explains what happens in writing, but suggests an aesthetic of true self-apparency for fiction. As Richard Rorty explains, "Writing is one of the representations of the trace in general, it is not the trace itself. *The trace does not exist.*" [17] Even "representation" is too strong; *trace* is the name for something that's defined by its absence, so what's being represented is *the lack of something* and not that thing in itself. Derrida himself "represents" it in language by crossing out the words which presume to make an identification—"the

sign ~~is~~ that ill-named ~~thing~~, the only one, that escapes the in-
stituting question of philosophy: what is . . . ?" (*Of Grammatology*, p. 19). Elsewhere he describes it as "somewhat like the architecture of an uninhabited or deserted city, reduced to its
skeleton by some catastrophe of nature or art."[18]

Derrida's approach to philosophy shares this same premise,
and suggests a self-apparent approach to writing. His tradition
is that of Hegel, not Kant, which means he disavows what Richard Rorty calls "a vertical relationship" between philosophic truth
and its representations in favor of treating truth horizontally—
"as the culminating reinterpretation of our predecessors' reinterpretation of their predecessors' reinterpretations. . . . This tradition does not ask how representations are related to nonrepre-
sentations, but how representations can be seen as hanging
together." Derrida's writing, like the self-apparent novel, is its
own reality. "It is the difference," Rorty concludes, "between
regarding truth, goodness, and beauty as eternal objects which
we try to locate and reveal, and regarding them as artifacts whose
fundamental design we often have to alter" (p. 143). Kant, like
Robbe-Grillet, believed the object (truth, or a thing) is "eter-
nally present to man's gaze"; his philosophy (and, we might add,
Robbe-Grillet's *nouveau roman*) lets us "see more clearly" (p. 144).
But for Derrida, "writing always leads to more writing" and
hence he "wants to keep the horizontal character of Hegel's notion of philosophy without its teleology, its sense of direction,
its seriousness" (p. 145).

Having writing represent only itself, and not some signified
meaning, carries profound implications for both fiction and philosophy, and Derrida's critique of writing in *De la grammatologie*
indicates just how things change under such circumstances. His
opening chapter, "The End of the Book and the Beginning of
Writing," describes a shift of even greater magnitude than Barthes'
epistemological break of 1850, though this latter disruption
functions as a part of the former. "Reading should free itself, at
least in its axis, from the classical categories of history," Derrida

begins (p. lxxxix), and the categories he refers to—including the logocentric origin of truth we have already discussed—span three thousand years of recorded Western history. Such logocentrism has debased writing, for it locates meaning in an eternal, ideal realm which writing only signifies. If writing is defined as "signifier of the signified," it will "conceal and erase itself in its own production" (p. 7)—the transparency of language which is as much a part of conventional fiction as it is of traditional Western metaphysics. For writing to be itself, the concept of the sign and the entire logic behind it must be destroyed, and it is to this purpose that *De la grammatologie* is dedicated.

Derrida's talk of "the history that has associated technics and logocentric metaphysics for nearly three millennia" and its current problematic state which "now seems to be approaching what is really its own *exhaustion*" within "this death of the civilization of the book" recalls the "death of the novel" and "literature of exhaustion" debates carried on by literary critics at this same time. This latter phenomenon was a critique of the traditional novel circa 1960, a claim that the conventional mimetic devices so useful to a world which valued morals and manners were becoming obsolete in an era whose behavior eclipsed the realms of belief. As Philip Roth himself, master of the signified reality, claimed:

> The American writer in the middle of the 20th Century has his hands full in trying to understand, and then describe, and then make *credible* much of the American reality. It stupefies, it sickens, it infuriates, and finally it is even a kind of embarrassment to one's own meager imagination. The actuality is continually outdoing our talents and the culture tosses up figures almost daily that are the envy of any novelist. [19]

The answer might be that culture, especially in the turbulent American 1960s, had readjusted its values beyond the conventions of traditional fiction. The world of signifiable order mandated by the conventional novel compares to the age of metaphysics described by Derrida, which is the ultimate grounding for the stable world of Philip Roth's preferred aesthetics.

> The difference between signified and signifier belongs in a profound and implicit way to the totality of the great epoch covered by the history of metaphysics, and in a more explicit and more systematically articulated way to the narrower epoch of Christian creationism and infinitism when these appropriate the resources of Greek conceptuality. (P. 13)

The religion of form which Ronald Sukenick believes constitutes the realistic novel enforces belief in the predictability of the world. "The key is verisimilitude: one can make an image of the real thing which, though not real, is such a persuasive likeness that it can represent our control over reality." It is Derrida and his *Tel Quel* colleague Julia Kristeva who identify this essential grounding of fiction (and of signifying language in general) within the structures of Platonic ideality and Christian faith. To Kristeva, the one-to-one identity between signifier and signified is based on the dominance of "God, Law, Definition." The terms of realism belong to "the 0–1 interval and are thus *monological*." Opposing this system (which Derrida calls the world of "the book," where meanings are ascribed to signifiers on an immediate basis) is Kristeva's disruptive literature. "The only discourse integrally to achieve the 0–2 poetic logic is that of the carnival" which rebels against the Law of God and substitutes something else.

> In fact, this "transgression" of linguistic, logical, and social codes within the carnivalesque only exists and succeeds, of course, because it accepts *another law*. Dialogism is not "freedom to say everything," it is a *dramatic* "banter" (Lautréamont), an *other* imperative than that of O. We should particularly emphasize this specificity of dialogue as *transgression giving itself a law* so as to radically and categorically distinguish it from the pseudo-transgression evident in a certain modern "erotic" and parodic literature. The latter, seeing itself as "libertine" and "relativizing," operates according to a principle of *law anticipating its own transgression*. It thus compensates for

monologism, does not displace the 0–1 interval, nor has anything to do with the architectonics of dialogism, which implies a categorical tearing from the norm and a relationship of nonexclusive opposites.[20]

Such writing described as "monological" includes "the representative mode of description and narration," "historical discourse," and "scientific discourse." "In all three, the subject both assumes and submits to the rule of 1 (God). The dialogue inherent in all discourse is smothered by a *prohibition*, a censorship, such that this discourse refuses to turn back upon itself, to enter into a dialogue with itself" (pp. 76–77). To disrupt laws of language based on this 0–1 interval, Kristeva says, "challenges God, authority, and social law" (p. 79). The epistemological break described by Barthes inaugurates, in fact, "the struggle against Christianity and its representations" (p. 80), representations upon which it depends for existence because, as Derrida concludes, "the intelligible face of the sign remains turned toward the word and the face of God" (*Of Grammatology*, p. 13).

"The sign and divinity have the same place and time of birth," Derrida insists. "The age of the sign is essentially theological," and our entire metaphysics makes the reading text a "fabric of signs . . . confined within secondariness. They are preceded by a truth, or a meaning already constituted by and within the element of the logos." Under Kant, writers do not write, they show. What happens, however, if there were "no linguistic sign before writing" (p. 14)? What happens to our world when reading changes to the point that "there is nothing outside of the text" (p. 158)?

If the idea of the book as "an accurate treatment of a subject" is to overcome, an entire metaphysics must be turned on its head. Richard Rorty emphasizes the dimensions of what Derrida proposes. *"He is suggesting how things might look if we did not have Kantian philosophy built into the fabric of our intellectual life, as his predecessors suggested how things might look if we did not have religion built into the fabric of our moral life.*" To deconstruct the text, to rid it of presupposed meanings, descriptions, representations, and the like, is really "to change ourselves" (Rorty, p. 149). Only by deconstructing the metaphysics of presence will texts be unburdened of the need to represent.

If there is nothing beyond the text, if words don't represent something nonlinguistic, then language is no longer a tool but rather "that in which we live and move" (Rorty, p. 150). Writing becomes primary, not secondary. The medieval ideal of the best writing as natural, eternal, and universal, representing God's truth, now yields to what this same age called *fallen writing*—that is, literature made of man's words, not God's. Presence, itself an ideal notion which posits a transcendental signified as the ultimate grounding for the difference between signifier and signified, is replaced by difference itself as a *trace* in the text. The structural poetics devised by Jonathan Culler makes use of this concrete, willful play of difference.

> The primary practical effect of this reorientation is to stress the active, productive nature of reading and writing and to eliminate notions of the literary work as "representation" and "expression." Interpretation is not a matter of recovering some meaning which lies behind the work and serves as a centre governing its structure; it is rather an attempt to participate in and observe the play of possible meanings to which the text gives full access. (*Structuralist Poetics*, p. 247).

Self-apparency, therefore, is much more than self-reference, for that reference is to the practice of writing (not to its functions) and is fully reflexive (and not just parodic). Much contemporary fiction calls itself innovative yet remains the favorite of conservative, Aristotelian critics precisely because it parodies the functions of writing without ever subverting or disrupting its traditional aims. The novels of John Barth and Thomas Pynchon, for example, use some of the referential techniques proposed by Derrida and Kristeva. Barth's *Chimera* (1972) employs narrators who question their own ability to write; Pynchon's

Gravity's Rainbow (1973) at times makes intricacies of plot and the plot-making urge its own subjects. Yet each writer is more the parodist than innovator, for Barth is presenting the imitation of an imitation of an action while Pynchon is simply ascribing human psychological qualities (such as paranoia) to equally portrayed behavior. *Chimera* and *Gravity's Rainbow* are ultimately dramas of the signified rather than self-referential performances of the signifier, for each depends upon a pass-through to certain represented objects. The technique is one of rhetoric, as Douglas R. Hofstadter demonstrates with certain parodic sentences: "This sentence is false," "This sentence no verb," "This sentence would be seven words long if it were six words shorter," and so forth."[21] In each case, it is the function of conventional writing (to signify some *thing*) which is parodied, and parody depends upon the object mocked for its own existence—indeed, it flatters the object. To practice writing is not to parody signifying, it is to destroy the very practice of signifying itself. Materiality of text is the product of this destruction, and makes reading an attractive and rewarding activity. "He who knows not language serves idols," warns Philippe Sollers; "he who could see his language would see his god."[22]

chapter 4   REFLEXIVE FICTION

"His writing is not *about* something," Samuel Beckett said of his mentor, James Joyce; "*it is that something itself.*"[1] Simply stated, this is the ideal of fictive self-apparency. But viewing literature in such a way can only take place with a monumental shift in the practice of aesthetic perceptions. An entire stage in appreciation must be altered; for when a literary work becomes an object in the world rather than a commentary or reflection, it must thereafter be encountered just as other objects already existing. As Donald Barthelme summarizes in his appropriately titled essay, "After Joyce," "The reader is not listening to an authoritative account of the world delivered by an expert (Faulkner on Mississippi, Hemingway on the corrida) but bumping into something that is *there*, like a rock or a refrigerator."[2] A proper response, then, is something quite different from the passive survey of secondhand reports. "The reader reconstitutes the work by his active participation," Barthelme indicates, "by approaching the object, tapping it, shaking it, holding it to his ear to hear the roaring within" (p. 14).

The world of self-apparent fiction is a world made anew. Fresh perception is necessary for creating it, but no less than the vitalistic sense of play each reader must bring to the work in its realization. Here is where self-reflexion makes the novel a two-way affair. "Play is one of the great possibilities of art," Barthelme counsels; "it is also, as Norman O. Brown makes clear in his *Life Against Death*, the Eros-principle whose repression means total calamity." For Barthelme, the authors of the *nouveau roman* lack this quality of play. "Their work seems leaden, self-conscious in the wrong way. Painfully slow-paced, with no leaps of the imagination, concentrating on the minutiae of consciousness, these novels scrupulously, in deadly earnest, parse out what can safely be said" (p. 16). The self-reflexion his American colleagues introduce is far more exuberant and oriented toward comic play.

Barthelme begins with the same theoretical dissatisfactions which bothered the French—he has said that he never thought fiction was possible until discovering Beckett—but his own style takes a more lively direction. What he calls the artist's effort to attain a fresh mode of cognition, Anaïs Nin formulates as a renewal of perception. Her *The Novel of the Future* argues that fiction is reconstructed reality: something added to the world, and more. "The writer shakes up the familiar scene, and as if by magic, we *see a new meaning in it*."[3] This renewed perception is somewhat like Shklovsky's process of defamiliarization, though Nin's effect is an alternately constructive/deconstructive affair. Her art is often that of subtraction—of having less say more, but in a uniquely compositional way. Her favorite illustration is Brancusi's sculpture, where "the expression of the flight of a bird was achieved by eliminating the wings" (p. 24). Clichés kill language, and with it perception, so Nin's fiction steadfastly avoids even the slightly obvious. What was "novel" in 1850 can hardly be surprising a century later, yet the old formulations persist, causing Nin to wonder.

> It is a curious anomaly that we listen to jazz, we look at modern paintings, we live in modern houses of modern designs, we travel in jet planes, yet we continue to read novels written in a tempo and style which is not of our time and not related to any of these influ-

ences. The new swift novel could match our modern life in speed, rhythms, condensation, abstraction, miniaturization, X rays of our secrets, a subjective gauge of external events. It could be born of Freud, Einstein, jazz, and science. (P. 29).

What these four elements have in common is a compositional self-consciousness, a self-apparency of system—a belief, in other words, that all descriptions are fictions (Heisenberg, Gödel), that behavior is a system of signs legible to readers of the subconscious (Freud), that all measurements are relative (Einstein, Saussure), and that process is more important and certainly less elusive than product (jazz). But for fiction to attain this degree of self-apparency, its major components would need to be recognized for what they were in themselves.

"It seems a country-headed thing to say," William H. Gass begins his essay on the medium of fiction, "that literature is language, that stories and the places and the people in them are merely made of words as chairs are made of smoothed sticks and sometimes of cloth or metal tubes." Because words *refer*, readers resist their own textuality for a different kind of pleasure. "It seems incredible, the ease with which we sink through books quite out of sight, pass clamorous pages into soundless dreams." Barthelme has cited the profundity of the shift from fiction as reportage to fiction as object, and Gass sympathetically agrees. "That novels should be made of words, and merely words, is shocking, really," he admits. "It's as though you had discovered that your wife were made of rubber: the bliss of all those years, the fears . . . from sponge."[4]

Gass advances Barthelme's and Nin's ideas of the creative role in fiction. "The artist's task is . . . twofold," he argues. "He must show or exhibit his world, and to do this he must actually make something, not merely describe something that might be made" (p. 8). When constructions are received according to the rules for descriptions, however, fiction reads awry. And when authors pander to this interest, they sacrifice the best in their art, forfeiting true creativity. "Novels in which the novelist has effaced himself," Gass propounds, "create worlds without gods"

(p. 20). The signs of fiction should not pass out of consciousness; they should remain and even sing for the readers who may return to them "again and again" (p. 31). But there remains that other, easier temptation, to pass through the page to a world we are pathetically eager to have exist. Out of this misreading is most conventional fiction produced.

Literary language, however, is not the same as the language used in real life; literature only mimics it, Gass suggests, indicating the root for this very fatal confusion which fictional self-reflection seeks to prevent. When mimicry is more obviously parody, M. M. Bakhtin insists, such mistakes are less inevitable. "The War Between the Mice and the Frogs," Bakhtin explains, is not written in the language of Homer; rather it is "an *image of the Homeric style*. It is precisely style that is the true hero of the work."[5] He argues that the novel as a genre is born of parody, of the laughter which discredits all authoritarian, dogmatic, "monological" structures by entertaining the opposing view—creating, in other words, a dialogue which focuses attention on the system rather than on the thing in itself. "Language in the novel not only represents, but itself serves as the object of representation. Novelistic discourse is always criticizing itself" (p. 49). Mimicry "rips the word away from its object, disunifies the two," Bakhtin explains, freeing language from its signifying process and letting it be itself (p. 55).

> These parodic-travestying forms prepared the ground for the novel in one very important, in fact decisive, respect. They liberated the object from the power of language in which it had become as if in a net; they destroyed the homogenizing power of myth over language; they freed consciousness from the power of the direct word, destroyed the thick walls that had imprisoned consciousness within its own discourse, within its own language. A distance arose between language and reality that was to prove an indispensable condition for authentically realistic forms of discourse. (P. 60)

Gass has his own name for this process: *metaphor*, which he calls "a form of presentation or display" (p. 63). When written well, metaphor becomes a process of sensuous exhibition, an organization which draws attention to itself as well as to its object of discourse. Certain writers such as Richard Brautigan and Tom Robbins stretch the distance between tenor and vehicle as far or even farther than reasonably possible; in addition to illuminating the object at hand, this method draws attention to the writer's act of comparison—indeed, often lavishing such pyrotechnics of language on the reader that the original object from the world is lost, to be replaced by something made of its author's language, as in these examples from Brautigan's *Trout Fishing in America* and Robbins' *Another Roadside Attraction*:

> Eventually the seasons would take care of their wooden names [on poor peoples' grave markers] like a sleepy short-order cook cracking eggs over a grill next to a railroad station. Whereas the well-to-do would have their names for a long time written on marble hors d'oeuvres like horses trotting up the fancy paths to the sky.[6]

> Man, Purcell has a grin like a beer barrel polka. A ding-dong daddy grin. A Brooklyn Dodger grin. A grin you would wear to a Polish wedding. His smile walks in in wooly socks and suspenders and asks to borrow the funny papers. You could trap rabbits with it. Teeth line up inside it like cartridges in a Mexican bandit's gunbelt. It is the skunk in his rosebush, the crack in his cathedral.[7]

In each case representation has yielded to metaphoric display; the gap between object and manner of expression is so wide that the reader pays more attention to the writer's daring act than to the qualified object. Simple description could have been dispatched in far fewer words; stacking them up this way only serves to emphasize the system of fiction—its process—at the expense of a functional report.

There is, of course, much human energy and imagination evident in these processes; like following the track of an abstract expressionist painter, the reader can relive the act of creating these words. Action painting, action writing—the process is the same, with emphasis less on the finished product than on the author's process of creation. "If metaphor is a sign of genius," Gass considers, "it is because, by means of metaphor, the artist is able to organize whole areas of human thought and feeling, and to organize them concretely, giving to his model the quality of sensuous display"; a reading of that process yields "a brand-new ordering both of the world and our understanding" (pp. 68–69). As Harold Rosenberg said of action painting, the canvas (or here writer's page) becomes less of a surface upon which to represent than an arena within which to act. Though figures may be discerned in an abstract expressionist work, it is a mistake to claim them as intended representations; likewise, as Gass insists, "In a metaphor that's meant, the descent to the literal can never be made" (p. 76). Deliberate strategies—Brautigan's far-out images, the length of Robbins' comparisons—frustrate such misreadings. The only way to appreciate their work is to flow with the play of language, each work's own proper subject.

In self-apparent fiction, the reader's attention is directed to language. But what of the author's responsibility to character, theme, and meaning—to the issues of "Humanism" as they have traditionally informed fiction? Self-apparent novels have been caught in a cross fire of contradictory interests, satisfying no one, for on the one hand the necessary referentiality of words seemingly limits their chance to be abstractly expressive, yet their very attempts at eluding reference anger the traditionalists who claim such fiction has abandoned life. John Gardner's *On Moral Fiction*[8] and Gerald Graff's *Literature Against Itself*[9] decry experiments toward self-apparency. "The medium of literary art is not language," Gardner claims, "but language plus the writer's experience and imagination" (p. 124). These two latter factors are expressed through dramatized imitation and reflection, as expected by readers, for "what chiefly interests us in fiction is characters in action" (p. 113). "Matter" is more important to Gardner than "manner" (p. 193), a strategy by which he dismisses not only recent American innovations but much of William Faulkner's work as well. The motive behind this is didactic. "Art, in short, asserts an ultimate rightness of things which it does not pretend to understand in the philosopher's way but which it nevertheless can understand and show mankind" (p. 173). "Note the scheme," Gardner tells us: "from God comes the standard; it is enacted by a hero and recorded by the poet" (p. 28).

Gerald Graff's position is even more critical. "The weakness of much postmodern fiction," he concludes, "lies in its inability or refusal to retain any moorings in social reality" (p. 209). For him, literary thinking is inseparable from its moral and social counterparts; and as he insisted in a symposium on reader-response criticism, messages encoded in a novel and at the bottom line of a bank statement were identical in the way they worked, for reader and for writer alike.[10] Like Gardner, Graff demands an external grounding (in the real world) for fiction; moreover, that ground must be one of authority, whether psychological or moral. Graff's colleague Frank D. McConnell goes even farther in dismissing fictional self-apparency by demanding that Tony Tanner's concept of the "City of Words" be replaced by St. Augustine's "City of God."[11] Contemporary innovations are what they are, Graff concludes, only because of social and cultural abnormalities, a theory also shared by Josephine Hendin, whose *Vulnerable People: A View of American Fiction Since 1945* outlines the pathology.

> Anarchic fiction [Thomas Pynchon] and holistic fiction [Robert Coover] represent distortions of the human situation which lead to different ends, the one toward the impersonality of mysticism, the other toward the impersonality of technology. Postwar fiction reflects a spirit of divergence in our time. It shows the deification of the uncontrollable, the random, the fragmentary, and the deification of the performer, of man as a success machine. Both bear witness to our fascination with vulnerability and power.[12]

Yet these very same arguments can be turned around, to make the argument that traditional fiction—by its allegiance to an outmoded ethic and aesthetic—has abandoned the cause it so loudly celebrates, and that contemporary innovations have, in fact, kept the most human elements in fiction alive and pertinent to our condition. Mas'ud Zavarzadeh describes these earlier forms as "totalizing novels," which are "fictional constructs which were by and large continuous with the structure of feelings and events in the empirical world."[13] These novels "functioned as paradigms of the experience of the times," letting the novelist "totalize various manifestations of life around him into rationally significant and mimetically recognizable microcosms." Representative fiction was thus appropriate to a Newtonian, objectively scientific, pre-Freudian world. To write novels by this rubric today, however, is (as Anaïs Nin has argued) a fundamentally dishonest affair. As Zavarzadeh accuses, "those who do so and attempt to totalize contemporary experience end up interpreting the present by reference to a preestablished code of values inherited from bygone days." "By inventing a myth of continuity based on an assumption of coherent external reality" these neo-traditionalists "lie to their readers as they give false assurances about a nonexistent order." These novelists "provide the readers with an escape from the incongruous realities of the times rather than exposing them to an imaginative exploration of such realities" (pp. 223–24).

Thematic escapism is matched by the damaging power of realistic techniques employed for the portrayal of essentially unrealistic experience. Signs—created signals which indicate particular configurations of experience in the world—are handy devices, which the realist can use as a type of shorthand to cue reader responses and hence simplify his work (and theirs). "Such signals assure us that we are here, oh yes, in the world we understand," Gilbert Sorrentino suggests, but what we really "understand," he concludes, "are the signals. . . . we think we are learning something, we are seeing 'beneath the surface' of things, but we are seeing nothing at all."[14] Signals only work at all because they tell the reader what he or she already knows; but when a fiction comes to be dominated by them—when they are the essential effect, as might happen in a story by John O'Hara or John Cheever—much of the aesthetic power is lost. "They allow the writer to slip out from under the problems that only confrontation with his materials can solve," Sorrentino argues. In fact, "Novels are made of words," and the art must happen there to be successful.

> The words must also have, in their composition, a texture and design we call style. The novel must exist outside of the life it deals with; it is not an imitation. The novel is an invention, something that is made; it is not the expression of "self"; it does not mirror reality. If it is any good at all it mirrors the processes of the real, but, being selective, makes a form that allows us to see these processes with clarity. Signals in novels obscure the actual—these signals are disguised as conversation, physiognomy, clothing, accouterments, possessions, social graces—they satisfy the desire that we be told what we already know, they enable the writer to manipulate his book so that it seems as if life really has form and meaning, while it is, of course, the writer who has given it these qualities. It is the novel, of itself, that must have form, and if it be honestly made we find, not the meaning of life, but a revelation of its actuality. We are not told what to think, but are instead directed to an essence, the observation of which leads to the freeing of our own imagination and to our arrival at the only "truth" that fiction possesses. The flash, the instant or cluster of meaning must be extrapolated from "the pageless actual" and presented in its imaginative qualities. The achievement of this makes a novel which is art: the rest is pastime. (Pp. 196–197)

To insist that fictive language tells the same truth in the same way as empirically referential talk denies that such language has a reality of its own, and that there might be any reason to read literature except for the puppet show of ideas and action its language depicts. By claiming their own reality, the words of fiction at once admit their own provisionality (after all, they are self-consciously created) and their imaginative avenue to the truth; only this way can there be freedom of action in a novel beyond that found in a biography or historical account. Only in this way, in fact, does fiction have any excuse for existing.

The best defense of self-apparent fiction can be found in a

series of essays written by novelist Ronald Sukenick. Variously titled "Digressions" toward a literary theory,[15] they are cut from the whole cloth of Sukenick's running battle with both the literary and academic establishments which prefer mimesis for its superior sales and moralistic teachability. This very ease in turning fiction into a movable product is itself grounds for suspicion, a reduction of artistic language to a summary of the concepts it conveys—or, in other words, bypassing the imaginative grace of a special signifying process in favor of the cut-and-dried message in "signifieds" themselves. Given the twentieth century's reluctance to verify the thing in itself apart from its creative processes, such "socially realistic" fiction is in fact a great illusion, for it claims that an unpredictable world is predictable indeed, that the mysterious forces of life are really under our control, and that a fabrication of the real can be so lifelike as to be substituted for the thing itself. That is voodoo, Sukenick argues: a fraudulent but necessary practice when the aims of fiction are not imaginative expression but readily marketable instruction.

Such reductive realism in fiction is self-contradictory, for the closer its language is to the signified object, the less it can be a sign in itself and hence profit by the materiality of its own artifice. Even in classic philosophical terms, the imitation set forth is only a Platonic shadow, a secondhand counterfeit which the true idealist should shun as inferior to the world of essences. Yet this may be what the realists want: a safe, inert form of art prophylactically isolated from the experiential flow of life. Self-apparent fiction, especially in its reflexive stage, shocks critics like Gardner and Graff because of its seeming crudity; if there are writers in the past to be scorned as much as the current innovationists, they would be Henry Miller, William Carlos Williams, and before them all Walt Whitman—writers who used personal experience on the same level as more conventionally artistic material. For Miller especially, the data of experience held equal status with the materials of art; indeed, he fashioned his own life as a work of fiction, calling on its sexual energies to provide the structuring force of his literary achievement. Here may be found the immediacy and authority for the self-apparent experiments of today, where the writer is directly responsible for his or her work.

Mimetic fiction as voodoo, trying to substitute the artificial for the real; mimesis itself as a way of abstracting art from life's energy—these are the negative elements of realism which Sukenick claims inhibit self-apparency. Behind it all is one's attitude toward words: do they mean the same in fictional works as they do in simple exposition? Gerald Graff claims they do. "I believe that literature," he insists, "does make truth claims, and makes them in the same way as non-literary statements do."[16] Sukenick counters by citing etymology. "The word *fog* in *Bleak House* does not mean the same thing as the word *fog* in the dictionary," he explains, "though its meaning in *Bleak House*, once developed, could be, probably has been, added to the general sense—one sees this process on any page of the *OED*" (*NLH* 6:434). Countering Graff's and Gardner's claims that literary words mean all the same thing is this innovation in sense and nuance as poets and novelists reshape language year by year from book to book.

On the positive side, Sukenick counts four major elements in innovative fiction's success, all linguistically self-apparent. First, rather than shunning the energy of life, fiction must express its experiential flow; indeed, like jazz and action painting, that flow often is not a single attribute but becomes the work itself. Which leads to his second point: the activity of composition is what draws us to the work, is what we watch and even what we re-create in our reading. Thirdly, this form of composition is the work's field of action, and its relative integrity and compositional success determines the work's merit. Finally, there is the measure of self-apparency which guarantees the work as valid.

As artifice the work of art is a conscious tautology in which there is always an implicit (and sometimes explicit) reference to its own nature as artifact—self-reflexive, not self-reflective. It is not an imitation but a new thing in its own right, an invention. (*PR*, p. 99).

The result is not simple self-expression, for the personal experience is simply treated like any other data from the world—no better, no less. What's emphasized is the artist at work, not the tortured genius of his soul. Fully banished is the "crystal perfection" of art, a fake idealism which only weakens fiction the better to enhance its moral teachability. A priori ideals yield to the chance of what might happen, a work of art which develops by digression: jazz, collage, action painting, self-apparent fiction. As for subject, the criterion John Gardner held above all others, Sukenick counters that "just as one cannot say that a piece of music is 'about' its melody, one should not say that a piece of fiction is 'about' its subject matter—subject matter is just one element of the composition" (*NLH* 6:433).

The leading contemporary theorists of fictive self-apparency are also its main practitioners. The short stories and novels of Donald Barthelme, William H. Gass, Ronald Sukenick, and Gilbert Sorrentino describe the form's development throughout the American 1960s and seventies—a radically creative time for arts and society as well—from Barthelme's *New Yorker* contributions (beginning in 1963) to Sorrentino's self-reflexive *tour de force*, the novel *Mulligan Stew* published in 1979.

Barthelme's stories have been a necessary first step in educating a popular readership to the new aesthetics of reflexive fiction. They are the most accessible, sometimes appearing as little more than comic routines on the order of Woody Allen, George Carlin, or David Steinberg. Yet the special popularity of this comic style (another sixties innovation) is part of the same cultural turnabout which created the market for reflexive fiction. Woody Allen makes fun of his posture as comedian; so do Barthelme's stories. A more traditional comic superiority or hauteur—that of Bob Hope, for example—yields to the humble effacement of Allen's bumbling style. Eventually, the aesthetic exhausts itself and becomes pure gesture, as in the self-consciously "bad" comedy of Steve Martin, whose lines are less humorous than the spectacle of the comedian himself putting on such a poor show. From Barthelme to Sorrentino self-reflexive fiction follows this same course, from the conscientious exuberance of "Me and Miss Mandible" and "Marie, Marie, Hold on Tight" to Sorrentino's depletion of these same techniques in *Mulligan Stew*, a self-consciously terrible novel which deliberately fails every test of good writing.

Donald Barthelme's earliest stories, some of which he prefers to remember as parodies and satires, consist of the most mechanically self-apparent substitutions. Three friends picket a church, protesting the spiritual waste of man's fate; a grown man suddenly finds himself returned to sixth grade, jammed into a child's desk and subjected to the most anguishing sexual fantasies for his teacher. Even more artificially constructed stories have their only action take place within language itself: the wacky phraseology of *Consumer Reports* testing, or the stilted affectation of New Wave film scenarios; one entire story, forty "chapters" long, is written in the ministyle form of *TV Guide* program notes.[17] Occasionally Barthelme ventures into more obvious self-apparency, as in the story "Sentence" which begins "Or a long sentence moving at a certain pace down the page aiming for the bottom" and continues for seven pages of self-description,[18] the Joycean word-salad of "Bone Bubbles" (which reads "double dekko balcony of a government building series of closeups of the food thread long thin room" and so forth),[19] or the spectacularly odd verbal constructions of his story "Paraguay,"[20] which he once named as his favorite and analyzed for a short-story anthologist.[21] In a symposium with William H. Gass and others Barthelme talked about experimenting with "the enormous resources of language,"[22] but his own preference is for the materiality of his craft, the physical nature of words on the page and the way one can tinker with them. Twice a magazine editor by profession, Barthelme admits "I enjoy editing and enjoy doing layout— problems of design. I could very cheerfully be a typographer."[23]

Many of his stories contain graphic collages in the manner of Max Ernst's novel, *Une semaine de bonté*. "A Nation of Wheels" draws clichés from conversation and illustrates their absurdity (and further brings their dead meaning back to life) by making appropriate collages of the material elements sloppy usage has killed.[24] Other stories are made purely of bantered conversation—verbal riffs tossed back and forth as if between jamming musicians, where the quality of language gets more rewarding attention than any search for meaning. Character, action, plot, theme, and even the directive presence of a narrator (there are no "he said"'s) are all removed, in favor of a story whose only active presence is language itself.

> —Momma didn't 'low no clarinet played in here.
> Unfortunately.
> —Momma.
> —Momma didn't 'low no clarinet played in here.
> Made me sad.
> —Momma was outside.
> —Momma was *very* outside.
> —Sitting there 'lowing and not-'lowing. In her old rocking chair.
> —"Lowing this, not-'lowing that.
> —Didn't 'low oboe.
> —Didn't 'low gitfiddle. Vibes.
> —Rock over your damn foot and bust it, you didn't pop to when she was 'lowing and not-'lowing.
> —Right. 'Course, she had all the grease.
> —True.
> —You wanted a little grease, like to buy a damn comic book or something, you had to go to Momma.
> —Sometimes yes, sometimes no. Her variously colored moods.
> . . . .
> —She had a lot on her mind. The chants. And Daddy, of course.
> —Let's not do Daddy today.[25]

The most typical Barthelme story, however, uses the principle of collage for all the elements of fiction, including narrative, plot, action, and character. Because each component remains itself even as it is combined into a new entity, the artist's reflexive act of creation is kept in mind. "Porcupines at the University" chooses several unlike items, never before combined—a college dean, a scout and two cowboys, a herd of porcupines—and mixes them together in a tightly sequential story. This forward action of narrative makes them interact; but in collage, each element retains its own material identity, so that like the head of George Washington pasted atop the body of Marilyn Monroe the artist's act of combination is always in the foreground, while the various parts of his composition keep their former identity as well:

> "And now the purple dust of twilight time / steals across the meadows of my heart," the Dean said.
>
> His pretty wife, Paula, extended her long graceful hands full of Negronis.
>
> A scout burst into the room, through the door. "Porcupines!" he shouted.
>
> "Porcupines what?" the Dean asked.
>
> "Thousands and thousands of them. Three miles down the road and comin' fast!"
>
> "Maybe they won't enroll," the Dean said. "Maybe they're just passing through."
>
> "You can't be sure," his wife said.
>
> "How do they look?" he asked the scout, who was pulling porcupine quills out of his ankles.
>
> "Well, you know. Like porcupines."[26]

Yet there are limits to Barthelme's self-reflexive fiction which halt its innovations short of complete linguistic self-apparency. His stories such as "Sentence" and "Bone Bubbles" are far less successful with his readership than even one like "Paraguay," whose word-play draws its humor at least partially from the referential content brought along. Barthelme's own preferences favor reference: his social fictions are often indistinguishable from his *New Yorker* "Comment" and parody pieces, all of which derive from the same satiric use of language the author makes himself or sees used around him. In the *New Yorker's* front pages "one can appear in Wednesday (when the magazine is generally avail-

able in New York) being mad about whatever one was overstim-
ulated by on Tuesday of the previous week," Barthelme writes in
the preface to his collected unsigned columns, *Here in the Village.*
"That is, there's a short lead time, almost as short as a daily
newspaper's, but still long enough to allow one to be angry in
tranquility."[27] Hence his motive is journalistic; despite the fact
that his subject is often the materiality of language, in Barthelme's hands it takes on satiric significance—making him one
of the leading social reporters of his day, because in the media-
conscious world of contemporary America so much reality *is* linguistic. Barthelme's innovations, therefore, may be less fictional
than representatively historical.

William H. Gass' novella, *Willie Masters' Lonesome Wife*,[28] is a
more obvious experiment in self-reflexivity. The inevitable product of a theorist who argues that fiction is language, it is the
story fiction itself can tell: "I am that lady language chose to
make her playhouse of." Yet Gass still must personify, and it is
one of the ironies of his work that although his words strive for
self-apparency, the very structure for this must be enclosed in
metaphor. In this case fiction is the lovely woman Babs (the text),
who is made love to (shaped into a novel) by a series of clumsy,
unappreciative lovers (writers who fail to realize the richly self-
apparent potential of language in their hands).

Yet the metaphor is made as physically real as possible, so that
at least the text itself will be apparent—there is no suspension
of disbelief here. Originally published as an oversized, unpagin-
ated paperback supplement to the *TriQuarterly* magazine, the
book's cover features the title-and-author graphics screened
frontally on a woman's nude body. The volume's back cover shows
the woman's backside, so that the work itself corresponds to a
woman's naked body about to be entered by the reader (who, as
is common in self-apparent fiction, acts by proxy for the author,
rehearsing his creation of the text). We soon learn that the woman
has a name and variously colored moods; to signal their changes,
Gass shifts from different shades and textures of paper for the

book's four succeeding sections. Babs herself never lets us forget her body (the cover model continues to strike various poses throughout the book, from eating capital letters of paragraphs to slinking around the page); her words are set in radically different typefaces, and on some pages she uses multiple columns to tell several stories at once. On two occasions her thoughtless lover, in this case Gass himself, has soiled the page with coffee-cup rings and ink stains. At all times we are reminded that there is a manuscript at hand. Occasionally Babs speaks pure poetry; at one point she plays with the physical sound of words apart from any meaning (as in "catafalque"). By the very end, Gass must use a rubber stamp to remind us that just the opposite effect of realistic fiction has transpired: instead of being swept away by the story's verisimilitude, "YOU HAVE FALLEN INTO ART—RETURN TO LIFE."

Is Gass writing self-apparent fiction? Like Barthelme's, his theory presents an almost perfect paradigm of language in the service of itself; but again like Barthelme, this theory propels itself to the goal with such force that certain elementary components of fiction are lost in the process. Donald Barthelme had wanted his fiction to be an object, an "itself" to be encountered in the world, to be "bumped into"; but in producing such fiction, he has often simply written social satire of such linguistic conditions already existing in contemporary American customs. William H. Gass also becomes more a reporter than a fictionist when he describes the philosophical mechanics behind fiction rather than using the conventions themselves in a self-apparent manner (this, we shall see, has been the achievement of Ronald Sukenick, only to be undercut by Gilbert Sorrentino). Is Gass a novelist or a philosopher? He has published works of each, and in texture and sense (the prime considerations in his theory of fiction) they are indistinguishable. First a representative paragraph from his "philosophical inquiry," *On Being Blue*:

> The common deer in its winter coat is said to be in the blue. To be in the blue is to be isolated and alone. To be sent to the blue room is to be sent into solitary, a chamber of confinement devoted

to the third degree. It's to be beaten by the police, or, if you are a metal, heated until the more refrangible rays predominate and the ore is stained like those razor blades the sky is sometimes said to be *as blue as*, for example, when you're suddenly adrift on a piece of cake or in a conversation feel a wind from outer space chill your teeth like a cube of ice. Ah, but what is form but a bum wipe anyhow? Let us move our minds as we must, for form was once only the schoolyard of a life, the simple boundary of a being who, pulsating like an artery, drew a dark line like Matisse drew always around its own pale breath. Blue oak. Blue poplar. Blue palm. There are no blue bugs of note, although there are blue carpenter bees, blue disk longhorn beetles, blue-winged wasteland grasshoppers, one kind of butterfly, bottle-fly, the bird, and not a single wasp or spider. The muff, the fur, the forest, and the grot.[29]

And another from *Willie Masters' Lonesome Wife*:

> Repetition is the essence of the comic because repetition is mechanical like love. Wheels and pistons, gears and cams are comical in themselves. Lying about on the garage floor, they can be the cause of giggles. Even the word, piston, is hilarious. Repeat rocker-arm, for instance—lug. Consider the nomenclature of the tool. Tools are terribly funny: monkey-wrench and hammer, pair of pliers. There are shafts, nuts, screws, and metal nipples. Our girl, the fat girl, me—I answer a knock on a doorway panel and who is it? It's the little mimsy-pimsy with the baggy mantles, dried and old and tired and still the dream of every male in the theatre because she's going to widen her walter for a him and he's going to find his leporello big as the bong of balboa in port au prince, and the girl asks who are you? Who are you, she says. I'm the pipe-fitter, he answers. Always, the house howls. Plainly machines have borrowed from the body all these names and all the body's functions. Now in those circumstances in which the essential humanity of the human has been called in question, in just those very circumstances, the height of humor has been scaled. . . . (olive section)

Each passage reflects Gass' theory: that words and sentences should refer less to an outside, signified reality, and more to themselves—whether in their individual physical sounds, or in the train of associations they build within the sentence or paragraph. In fact, according to Gass' theory of self-apparency, the earlier philosophic passage is more qualitatively fictional than the second, from his novella. And in each case, the meandering associations are conceptual, triggered by words of course which are first of all there for their self-apparent sense (deer in winter, isolation, confinement, punishment, beating, heating, and so forth) but which for action depend upon intellectual content, which takes us back from fictional self-apparency into philosophical debate. Gass' theory, then, does not provide the rubrics for fiction at all. Instead, it *is* his fiction itself—for the author a valid work of art, but utterly irreproducible for fiction at large.

When Donald Barthelme stretches his style of fiction to its logical conclusion, he winds up discarding every convention except dialogue itself—to him, the example of fiction existing within its verbal self, as if whenever we speak we create a fiction. William H. Gass reduces even farther, purging dialogue in favor of the speaker's monologue, which we've seen is often indistinguishable from philosophic speculation (just as Barthelme's column-chatter parodies cannot be distinguished in manner or method from his signed stories in the same magazine). Ronald Sukenick, whose theory is more prolific and embattled than Barthelme's or Gass', actually stays closer to the conventions of traditional fiction in his own novels and stories, most likely because his combative sense tells him here is where the contest must be fought. After all, the most common complaint against self-apparent fiction is that it lacks all the things which make for reader interest: character, plot, theme, and so forth. Can these devices be made to work for the self-apparent writer, rather than against him? Is there a way to still have representable action without losing the reader's attention as it drifts from the page to wander among the world's significations?

Sukenick's first solution was to integrate the act of creating fiction with the finished product of the novel itself. As one reads *Up*,[30] the activities of character and of author merge, and what we see from page to page is Ronald Sukenick writing and existing in his novel. There will often be a common stimulus to action, such as the author's unheated apartment causing him to write a passage in which his character, also named Ron Sukenick, is jailed in a freezing cell. Just as readers are prone to trace significations to their real-life equivalents, so too are they tempted to assume autobiographical influences for everything that happens in fiction. Rather than fight this impulse, Sukenick makes it part of his story. In creating this novel he is quite literally creating himself, according to the same subjectively projective ethic he described in his *Wallace Stevens, Musing the Obscure*. "When through the imagination, the ego manages to reconcile reality with its own needs, the formerly insipid landscape is infused with the ego's emotion; and reality, since it now seems intensely relevant to the ego, suddenly seems more real."[31] When author Ron Sukenick feels threatened, he runs his character through a dose of paranoia, according to the stock literary clichés cullable from Kafka, Orwell, and Céline. Inferiority is countered through the creation of a macho alter-ego:

> Strop Banally
> blond, tanned, well-tailored, and baritoned, football build, strength and regularity of feature
> (the time he spiked a sorority's spring party punch with Spanish fly, made boat fare to Europe selling old Dewey buttons, taught on several campuses without so much as a B.A., hit 100 on the Pasadena Freeway and talked the cop out of a ticket, posed as an artist in Paris and had a successful show without paintings, screwed in one household within twenty-four hours twin sisters simultaneously, and serially their mother, their old governess and an anonymous lady who had the wrong address, as well as at one time and place or another a countless assortment of sacrifices to a lust whose enormity demands memorial) (P. 4)

Sukenick can be reflective too, refusing to be caught up in the illusion of his own story—at one point he includes a newspaper review of this same Strop Banally novel he's writing. Writing and reacting become the same act: midway through the novel Sukenick stops by another character's apartment to discuss a scene they share, and when faced with the complaint that such behavior violates verisimilitude, counters: "Why should he have to suspend disbelief? It's all words and nothing but words. Are we children reading fairy tales or men trying to work out the essentials of our fate?" In addition, he must admit that a crucial linking scene has been lost, left in a book he returned to the library (pp. 222–23). This integration of life and art, Sukenick argues, is the key to his aesthetic: the energy of experience creates a vitalistic sense of composition, making fiction simply the purest form of life itself, rather than an idealized abstraction. His novella "The Death of the Novel"[32] works the same way, with lecture notes on contemporary fiction blending into the distractions of a class lecture, which in turn becomes indistinguishable from the extra-curricular activity its narrator (as always named "Ronald Sukenick") is undertaking. Both novel and novella end as the author writes his last manuscript page. The life of fiction has been that of its own creation, and now that book and story are done, the author wonders what he will do. Why not have a farewell party for his characters? How about introducing his fantasies to their real-life inspirations? Sukenick's joy is in the mechanics of fiction, even to the point of seizing all of realism's liabilities for misreading and using them as self-apparent conventions for his own literary work.

There can be only one *Up* and one "The Death of the Novel," however. Turning these conventions on their head, having the substance of fiction being the act of the author writing it, is a revolutionary gesture makable only once. Sukenick's subsequent work has moved on to other disciplines of form, as if writing a classic self-reflexive novel was just one choice from any number of experiments available. His novel *Out* (Chicago: Swallow Press, 1973) features no self-present writer at all; characters themselves change names and identities in a kaleidoscope of actions, and theme itself seems less important than the physical presence of the book itself. *Out* hands the business of self-apparency directly to the reader, for on no page (as opposed to the "readerly" sections of *Up*) can one get lost in the story. For one thing, the chapters are numbered backwards, from ten through nine-eight-seven down to zero, as if in a countdown for blast-off. The chapters themselves are printed differently: units of ten lines of type for chapter 10, followed by nine lines of type matched by one line of space in chapter 9, then eight lines of type versus two lines of blankness in chapter 8, and so on until chapter 1 presents a single typeset line for every nine lines of emptiness. The reader is physically aware of this progression, for the book is becoming faster and faster to read, until by the final chapter, 0, the pages turn completely blank and the reader is shot out of the end like a cannon ball. The novel's action suits this physical sense, as the protagonist journeys from the clutter and confinement of the urban East Coast through the opening spaces of the Midwest and Great Plains to the pure emptiness off the California shore.

Readers might object that Sukenick has turned self-reflection into silly gimickery, but in essence his technique is simply a discipline of self-apparency: to make both reader and writer aware of the limits of form, as in the metric and rhyming requirements of a sonnet, so that the reader's attention is kept on artifice as well as message and so that the writer must be constructively self-conscious as he or she decides what can go on the page. American fiction of the 1970s is rife with such disciplinary forms. Sukenick uses certain options of spacing lines on the printed page; his colleague Raymond Federman uses an even more mechanical form, the typewriter, to write one novel in the form of spatially arranged pages, each its own form (*Double or Nothing* [Chicago: Swallow Press, 1971]) and another with sections as perfectly justified typescript (*Take It or Leave It* [New York: Fiction Collective, 1976]), in which a writer-for-hire of overblown "French" love letters is forced to search for bizarre synonyms because each line must be exactly sixty letters and spaces long. Gilbert Sorrentino and Walter Abish have used the alphabet as formal structure for their respective novels *Splendide-Hotel* (New York: New Directions, 1973) and *Alphabetical Africa* (New York:

New Directions, 1974). Sorrentino's brief book takes its twenty-six chapter titles from the alphabet's succeeding letters; each title then becomes a provocation of what to write, whether it be of As on the printed page looking like flies breeding in decay, a "C Note" used to pay the debts of chapter three, or the base-ball scorer's delight in the symbology of the sports headline, "K-K-Koufax!!!" The only action evident in these chapters is the author's inspiration to write, much like Gass' dalliance on the color blue in his own philosophical speculations.

Abish's novel uses the conventions of fiction more energeti-cally, for characters, plot, theme, and action to wend their way through his alphabetically-titled chapters, albeit within the confines of a discipline more rigorous than any of his colleagues have dared. Chapter A, the first, uses only words beginning with the letter A; as one might suspect, the reading is anything but smooth, and the story's action must fight desperately to be ex-pressed. In chapter B, words beginning with that letter are added to the store; likewise for chapters C, D, E, and so forth, until little by little the entire alphabet becomes available. The reader, of course, is kept painfully aware of the rigors of composition at every step, so there is little danger of letting the action walk off the page. But the artificial structure of a developing novel is also made self-apparent, for there can be no first-person narrator un-til chapter I, the Queen cannot make her first appearance until chapter Q, and the rendezvous in Jedda must wait until chapter J. Rather than banish conventions, as does Sorrentino, Abish revels in them as tests against his novel's alphabetic limits. By chapter Z it would seem he is writing a fully conventional book, with no restraints at all, but at this point he is only halfway done. Twenty-six more chapters follow, marking backwards this time from Z, Y, and X down through C, B, and A, with words of those letters disappearing as each chapter makes its second, departing appearance. Characters, places, and narrative perspec-tives drop out by one, just as the novel's easy readability dissi-pates with the contraction of linguistic possibilities. Abish's own theory comes from Wittgenstein, that at the heart of all human problems are concerns with language. Running his readers through the expanding and contracting possibilities of *Alphabetical Africa* is a model of just how thoroughly language can effect behavior.

Drawing the reader's attention to conventions as conventions, and not simply to the posture of a writer composing a novel, has been the favored way for self-reflexive fiction to grow from the sterility of a single revolutionary act into a profitable mode of fiction. Robert Coover's *The Universal Baseball Association, Inc., J. Henry Waugh, Proprietor* (New York: Random House, 1968) adopts the style of "Magic Realism" developed by several South American writers to actively involve the reader in several self-reflexive actions of his story. Here there is no writer writing a novel; instead, Coover opts for mimesis by portraying a lonely middle-aged man who fills his time by devising and playing an intricate card-table baseball game, complete with personal averages, team statistics, and league histories. Henry Waugh, in effect, is creating characters and devising plots for their exercise, just as might any conventionally realistic author. Coover, however, shows us both sides of the story: Henry Waugh creating this world, but also the players living in it from their own point of view. Complications result when Henry's interests conflict with the necessary rhythm of life created for his players, making the book's action a self-reflexive affair involving the mechanics of storytelling. The reader is free to believe or to analyze at will, yet at all times knowing that it's the metafictional process which is making things happen.

South American writers have been doing this for decades. Julio Cortázar's story "Continuity of Parks" starts with an armchair reader beginning the story of a murderer in flight, a progress which brings the culprit through several scenes to the very room in which the reader is reading, there to commit another act most foul. Jorge Luis Borges writes in "The Circular Ruins" about a character trying to dream a man into existence, only to conclude that he himself is the product of someone else's dream. European writers also delight in the fiction-making process, from Peter Handke's rehearsals of the semiotic process in *Die Angst des Tormanns beim Elfmeter* (Frankfurt: Suhrkamp, 1970), translated as *The Goalie's Anxiety at the Penalty Kick* (New York: Farrar, Straus & Giroux, 1972) to Italo Calvino's play with the supposed device of signatures from different books mistakenly sewn into one volume and two readers' attempts to assemble the full story, *Se una notte d'inverno un viaggiatore* (Turin: Giulio Einaudi Editore, 1979), translated as *If On a Winter's Night a Traveler* (New York: Harcourt Brace Jovanovich, 1981).

Yet if the final outcome of self-reflection is metafiction, this style of novel would indeed be limited, and subject to conservative complaints that the great reflective scope of fiction has been narrowed to a contemplation of its own function—as if cars and airplanes no longer transported people or even demonstrated great innovations of design, but instead just dully existed for themselves. The best self-reflexive stories, like William H. Gass' philosophical propositions, are finally arguments only for themselves, and once repeated in great numbers become simply drones. Moreover, the question of whether fiction can bear the weight of meaning is sidestepped entirely; when discourse is so privileged, content becomes trivialized, a dismal state indeed. Gilbert Sorrentino's massive *Mulligan Stew* (New York: Grove Press, 1979) is proof that metafiction can go on forever without recourse to even a shred of meaning. What begins as a poorly written detective novel soon turns into the author's journal, notebooks, letters, and reviews; before long his characters keep diaries and exchange notes, and eventually write their own novel in which the original author is held captive. *Mulligan Stew* accomplishes nothing but the complete exhaustion of self-reflexive techniques as they were evolved in the 1960s, albeit in a hilariously entertaining way.

Is there a way that the conventions of fiction can be used in and of themselves, yet still be more than reductive, self-reflexive exercises? And can the problematics of a writer composing the novel at hand be made more interesting than a mere trick with mirrors—can that act also be the vehicle of meaning, interest, and even sympathy? Fiction written in the decade after the great North and South American innovations of 1960s indicates what a self-awareness of not just fiction but of fiction's innovations can achieve. Clarence Major's early novels, *All-Night Visitors* and *NO*, are crafted in the experimental style pioneered by Barthelme, Sukenick, and Gass. His mature work, however, which includes *Reflex and Bone Structure* and *Emergency Exit*, stands as distant from Sukenick as Sukenick's first experiments do from the more realistic fiction of the 1950s. In this second wave of innovation, moving beyond the one-shot revolutionary gestures of novelistic self-reflection, may fully self-apparent fiction be found.

chapter 5   THE SELF-APPARENT WORD

As the progression of the arts in the twentieth century, from action painting and nonpredictable music to anti-illusionistic theater, has moved through the effacement of subject matter toward an abstractly expressive focus on process, the conflicts over self-apparency have led to a crisis unique for writing. Words themselves are referential, and as the building blocks of fiction they seem inevitably to direct attention away from the page. Moreover, moralist critics and teachers argue that fiction exists in represented action, within the drama of characters and events which constitute its true subject. We have seen how that beginning in the mid 1960s American writers took heart from the innovations of their international colleagues (John Barth citing Jorge Luis Borges, Raymond Federman working on Samuel Beckett, Ronald Sukenick studying in Paris, Robert Coover introducing lesser known South American writers to the review journals and their readers) and began to push toward a linguistic self-apparency of both content and form, leading to experiments with reflexive fiction. This very form, however, with its bullish proclamation of aesthetic self-sufficiency, led to tautologies of style and left the genre vulnerable to the most simpleminded moralistic criticisms. Human interests still needed to be answered.

American writers emerging in the 1970s, a decade after the first pyrotechnics of reflexive experimentation, have been able to address these humane concerns more directly. Walter Abish, Stephen Dixon, and Clarence Major are distinguished by the success of their strategies for dealing with the life of the writer, of his techniques, and of his content. In their hands fiction has become once more a living, moving document. Only now this sense of vitality comes from its art of composition, rather than from the elements of story it represents. Addressing themselves in turn to each component of the literary process, Abish, Dixon, and Major show how at every step a self-apparency of concern invests writing with the richness of human imagination at work.

Walter Abish's fiction is exceptional for its awareness of the author's role in composition. As we have seen in chapter four, his first novel, *Alphabetical Africa*, is structured on the writer's principles of word-selection, the most basic act in presenting a story. With chapters named for the succeeding letters of the alphabet the author is reminded at every stage of his controlling form. In similar manner for the reader, the story cannot lose itself in projected illusions, for as soon as the alphabet expands to allow virtually free combinations of linguistic elements the writer turns his structure around and concludes with chapters in reverse alphabetical order. Here the self-apparency is even more extreme, for the reader must bid farewell to familiar persons, places, and things as their initial letters vanish into the history of Abish's composition.

Alphabetical Africa thus distinguishes itself by a self-apparency of form which is visible and operative on every page. The book can even be said to have its own life, an energetic breathing-in and breathing-out as the alphabetical possibilities in turn expand and contract. But there is a living writer who stands behind this fiction, and in a series of essays Abish has explored these highly personal concerns. "In a sense, the text is the writer's skin," Abish suggests, "the outermost delineation of his sensibility, his way of expressing, remembering and furiously rendering what he believes to be the exactitude of his feelings." As the pages of his manuscript accumulate, they become "an extension of the writer's nervous system, and his fingerprints on the pages testify to this nervous proximity, this incestuous intimacy to the text, or to be more precise, to the text-to-be." Most importantly, the writer's belief that "everything, literally everything he experiences can be accurately transferred onto paper" encourages the belief that "for everything under the sun there is a corresponding sign or word, and that the intensity of his ardor, his passion for life, will impress upon the pages the determination of his new commitment."[1] Control of these signs is thus a simulation of life—not for the text, as in illusionistic realism, but for the writer himself. I write, therefore I am.

Abish deliberately characterizes his author figure as "The Writer-to-Be"; before he finds the signs by which he extends his personhood, he does not exist as writer. Once in action, however, he does not simply range through the world's representations—not unless, however, he wishes to be a conventionally illusionistic writer of realism. For the author of *Alphabetical Africa*, the conditions are quite different. He will of course be drawn to "the familiar," but that very judgment is an index of his creative capabilities. What is familiar to one may not be so to another. As Abish observes in his paper "On Aspects of the Familiar World as Perceived in Everyday Life and Literature":[2]

> In viewing life as "familiar" the "self" not only embraces life and thereby attempts to affirm its identity, it also establishes a link to what it considers a desirable as opposed to a fearful and terrifying "otherness". . . . Only the sensational, the disasters, remain apart, unabsorbed, unassimilable by the "familiar" . . . yet, even those outrageous events, the Mylai massacre, the Jonestown killings, are provided with interpretations that demystify and reduce the horror to an impersonal "otherness": an impersonal "otherness" conveying not a personal threat to a certain "self" but a universal menace from which no one "self" can consider itself immune. (Pp. 1–2)

For the Writer-in-Action, the world is regarded "as an extension of its very being and its vocabulary" (p. 2)—hence the self-

apparent structure of *Alphabetical Africa* which called attention
to the self-imposed and artificial selection of literally every word
in the novel. Above all, the textual world is an expansion of self
and not a representation of other. "The 'familiar' is after all a
means of surviving the terror" of otherness, Abish insists. "Hence,
the need to see the world *familiarly* is the result of a preoccupation with the 'self' rather than with the world. The 'familiar' is
to be equated with 'self' preoccupation" (p. 3). The familiar world
is not discovered; instead, "We design it, we assemble it" (p. 8).
But once so designed, the text assumes its own vitality, suggesting the exaltation of the present Abish finds articulated by Jür-
gen Habermas. "The new value placed on the transitory, the elusive, and the ephemeral, the very celebration of dynamism,
discloses the longing for an undefiled, an immaculate and stable
present" (p. 12).

This rarified state is the life of fiction which Abish sees as
superior to earlier romantic posturings. "The contemporary author's major triumph," he notes, "has been his newfound ability
to free himself from the overriding demands of the 'self'—to
cease to pay the revered 'self' any further special attention" (p.
12). The writer's self now lives in his fiction. A superficially
realistic novel such as Abish's *How German Is It*[3] employs a pains-
taking observation of foreign details simply so that the realm of
the familiar may be established and hence assume its own textual
life. There is no "Germany" in the novel except as exists in Abish's
carefully selected signs; deliberate in their examination of surface qualities, they distinguish themselves by their identifying
function and so resist being swept up into any narrative effacement. As will be noted in chapter six, Abish uses the conventions of realism in a new, experimental way: describing in mi-
nute detail endless sequences of actions, including the everyday
encounters with social customs and changes in the weather, but
leaving major events virtually untouched in the background.

For writers of the self-apparent word, documentation exists
but takes place within the fields of language, not represented
reality. "An individual will use language to give shape to his *I*,"

Abish notes after examining the wealth of documents in his possession (passport, marriage license, driving license, bankbook,
credit cards). This is the beginning of his "Self-Portrait,"[4] the
model for a future book-length treatise on the constructive attributes of a writer's language. Although the documents mentioned are signifiers, the "I" they signify is never present within
them. It is present, however, in language, as part of the signifier-
signified nexus which creates the *sign*, yielding a great advantage.

> Language unlike a document permits the *I* to unfold, gives it a
> freedom to seek out the words that will define its intention and
> direction. It does not take long for an individual to discover that
> there is no need to stress the *I* when saying: I choose not to, or, I
> couldn't care less, or, I intend to take a walk around the park with
> out you. The recipient of the remark is able to place the *I* address
> ing him in a proper perspective. Not to be overlooked in some
> tortured statement is an *I* that stands in a state of solitary and
> nervous uncertainty in regard to the words that have preceded it
> and to words that are to follow. This precarious state of uncertainty
> is sufficient to crush the *I*, to obliterate it temporarily. (Pp. 1–2)

First-person singular thus enjoys greater advantages in writing than in life, as long as the *I* remains in control of its sentence. After all, "the moment the *I* is inserted in a sentence, the
recipient of the statement or remark is being led somewhere" (p.
2). This sense of creativity can be shared by the reader, again
thanks to the uniquely vitalistic properties of the word as sign.

> Frequently the reader, as if participating in a Pavlovian experiment,
> responds not to the story or novel, but to a word or sentence that
> catches his eye. Almost invariably the pronoun *she* precedes or closely
> follows the word or sentence which in the reader's brain has ac
> quired a highly charged content. Quite unknowingly the writer has
> provided the reader with an item of information that is self-contained,
> that can be lifted from the book, permitting the reader to linger
> over it as he forms his own anticipatory creation, a fantasy that
> functions independent of the story or book that initially was its
> raison d'être. (P. 8)

Are signs therefore superior to the real world? Abish need not venture so far as to assert this, and neither is it the pertinent question. Instead, suffice it to say that the unique capabilities of signs allows the writer to create a text which functions quite practically as its own world, with all the energy and intense interest as we are accustomed to find in life.

Walter Abish's fiction in general follows Wittgenstein's proposition that all philosophical problems (that is, all problems in life) are ultimately problems in language. The focus of activity in any Abish novel or story is therefore language, and his genius has been to make this play of words and syntax as interesting as the dance of illusions which conventional realists use to elicit human concern. Abish's texts demonstrate how matters of behavior are linguistically constructed—a fascination with key words and combinatory possibilities dominates many of his shorter works, and the social structures which language can produce form the substance of his novels and novellas.

The novella "This Is Not a Film. This Is a Precise Act of Disbelief" forms the centerpiece to the author's first collection, *Minds Meet*.[5] How we live, what our needs may be, and the form our hopes will take are all determined by the available surface of things surrounding us, this piece of fiction argues. Strongly narrative in form, it uses the methods of city planning (the trade which brought Abish to America after living in Austria, China, Israel, and England) to show how the structures available to us actually create, rather than serve, our needs. The occasion is the planning of a new shopping mall, which a French film director very much like Jean-Luc Godard[6] has come to study as an example of decadent American capitalism. The mall developer is part of a group which runs the town; within its population can be found a network of relationships, financial and sexual, which determine how things will happen. "This is a familiar world," the novella begins, announcing a strategy parallel to Abish's theory in "On Aspects of the Familiar World as Perceived in Everyday Life and Literature" and just as systematic as the alphabet in

Alphabetical Africa. "It is a world crowded with familiar faces and events. Thanks to language the brain can digest, piece by piece, what has occurred and what may yet occur" (p. 31). The developers plan malls, and the builders construct them according to plan—a comfortable arrangement of surfaces. The lowest worker in the story takes delight in forklifting cases of soda pop from shelves in the warehouse to pallets in the parking lot. (He also enjoys table tennis, just as his bosses enjoy bouncing their designs along the town's surface.) Disruptions of routine are moved aside, whether it be a retarded child shunted off to an institution or a corpse hidden behind locked doors. Whatever might be hidden beneath this clean and shiny surface is as important to Abish's work as to Poe's, and is a recurrent device to suggest how the systems which regulate our surface lives screen the less workable complications within the depths.

Much of *Minds Meet*, however, is playfully comic, toying with the inadequacies of a bumbling narrator. In "The Istanbul Papers" he is an embassy official seduced into giving Hitler's daughter a visa to the United States. "The Second Leg" finds this same type of figure as the odd-man-out at his girlfriend's apartment, where he plots out the doings in syntactic fashion.

> All evening I master forebearance. I decline to inquire into their true relationship, Why should it matter to me, a kind of stretched-out week-end guest, what she and Victor do in the bathroom. It is so simple to jump to an erroneous conclusion. First Victor excuses himself, and leaves the table. Then she goes to the kitchen to fetch the dessert and coffee. Don't run off and desert me, I say jokingly. The next thing I hear is their boisterous shouts, their unabashed shrill laughter. They do nothing to restrain their mirth . . . or the sound of running water. It is seeping through from under the bathroom door when I get up to investigate. I keep myself in check and do not bring it to their attention. All things considered . . . not to overlook the soaked bedroom slippers, as well as the inexplicable presence of the two damp pillows on the toilet seat. I am at an utter loss for an explanation. Is this all being done for my exclusive benefit? I am resolved not to take too dark a view of all this horseplay. (P. 111)

Still other stories verge on abstraction, as in "With Bill in the Desert" and "Non-Site." In the former piece a desert trek seems to be taking place in a small room lit by an unshaded bulb, Abish's fictive reaction to a work of conceptual art by Terry Fox where "the light formed a topography of the interior that was, at once, a familiar romantic configuration in which the tent became the emotive key to a kind of disturbance of things past, and another in which one's physical presence, one's emotions, were measured (and partly activated) by one's proximity to that light" (p. 103). It is in such conceptual artwork that Abish finds the true connection between surface and depth and indicates the direction his own work pursues.

In the Future Perfect,[7] Abish's second collection, shows the wide range of the author's methods, from the sign-fixated topology of "The English Garden" (which anticipates *How German Is It*) to a series of shorter pieces which experiment with structural forms even more complexly determining than that of *Alphabetical Africa*. In "Ardor / Awe / Atrocity," for example, block paragraphs are titled by a trinity of alphabetically ordered words, seventy-eight in all, which are in turn identified by superscript numbers (of their ordinal ranking according to the alphabet). The subtitles introduce us to the words before their narrative sense, and their superscription when they do appear reminds us that they are first of all lexical devices and only secondly signifiers of another reality. The story line itself discusses the surface of the "perpetual present" along which Californians propel themselves, acquiring styles from hit TV shows and acting them out along the boulevards, freeways, and beaches of their streamlined land. Without such shows as guidance, the story insists, the land and its people would be bereft of distinction. Citing the private detective hero, Abish notes that "keeping an eye on Mannix is one way of watching the smoothly functioning process of a culture prepared for any eventuality" (p. 49), as if the entire world has been converted to a movie screen. Breaking down this technique even further in the story "In So Many Words," Abish titles his paragraphs by the number of words they contain, and then mixes the contents up before repeating them in proper order. Hence the reader again encounters the words apart from any combinatory meaning; and even when the meaning emerges on the second reading through, there will still be a sense of each word's individuality remaining from the first self-apparent encounter. In similar manner the emerging story features a young woman around whom meaning slowly takes shape as the sense of her syntax forms itself: "They know nothing about her except what is on view. What is on view is splendidly displayed. It is, furthermore, on view in order to be appreciated" (p. 94), and that act of appreciation must be constructed according to rules of visual grammar, just as Abish unscrambles each paragraph's words to make sense.

Three of Abish's more recent stories are even more radical in their methods of self-apparency. Prefacing the first, Abish explains his intent.

> In constructing *Inside Out* I pretended that all books published in English represented a vast dictionary that made sentences (instead of just words) available to a writer. More or less at random I selected one sentence, and sometimes part of a sentence, from eighty authors. The numbers on the page indicate the number of words taken (and I cannot think of a more appropriate word) from each writer. The selection of the sentence, the sequence I followed and the idea to undertake this exercise are mine, but the story . . . ?[8]

The piece which follows does have a sense of progression to it, as a narrator describes his position, activities, and reactions— all of which is amazing because we have been told first off that the author has not composed these sentences but chosen them at random. This method is less shocking when we are reminded that there are such things as dictionaries of symbols which writers may use to create stories and which critics may in turn refer to for interpretation. But Abish's achievement is considerable when we note that words lose their self-apparency (and had in fact in his earlier experiments) just at the point of their combination into sentences. In "Inside Out" and the author's other variations in this mode the sense of opaqueness is expanded to include the sentence and then the paragraph, all the while maintaining a humanly interesting story.

"Ninety-Nine: The New Meaning"[9] and "What Else"[10] show Abish perfecting his theory and also moving toward longer selections, so that a fully new meaning for each sentence may be assumed from its new context. The first consists of ninety-nine selections each from page ninety-nine of books available in Abish's library, including two of his own. "What Else" allows the freedom of scanning fifty other books for passages that seem to be of use, although the story does not assume final form until all the selections are placed in Abish's "order." Such a technique—using others' sentences rather than his own—would seem to be the extreme of abstraction in composition. But Abish's device in fact produces the opposite effect, for so rich are words and their associations that even plucked so randomly they still allow the author to compose with great human significance. "What tense would you choose to live in?" this latter story concludes, and answers: "I want to live in the imperative of the future passive participle—in the 'what ought to be.' I like to breathe that way. That's what I like. It suggests a kind of mounted, bandit-like equestrian honor" (p. 119), much like the sense of vitality Abish's work entails.

This sense of creative enthusiasm for the act of writing—an ability to invest even the most mechanical of combinatory schemes with surprise and excitement—is extended to the techniques of fiction by Stephen Dixon. The author of two novels and over one hundred and fifty published stories (the best of them filling six collections), Dixon manages to take the most familiar and even overexploited conventions and reinvest them with a sense of novelty unknown within contemporary realism. His own sense of playfulness expresses itself in titles and structures, as in his volume *14 Stories*[11] which contains only thirteen pieces but whose first, "14 Stories," takes place on the thirteenth story of a hotel—which is, in common superstitious practice, designated as the fourteenth floor. Dixon's sense of artful whimsy helps structure the story, which begins where a conventional tale might end. "Eugene Randall held the gun in front of his mouth and fired. The bullet smashed his upper front teeth, left his head through the back of his jaw, pierced an ear lobe and broke a window that overlooked much of the midtown area" (p. 1). Already the reader has been told more about the shell's trajectory, by which the story's line of action will proceed, than about poor Eugene; but the tacky signs and symbols of his worldly life have been worked to death by realistic fiction, while the path of that utterly improbable bullet opens the way to genuinely interesting material.

The gun's sound has penetrated several floors of the hotel, alerting a maid; one of his suicide notes has drifted out the broken window; and the bullet itself lands a block away on a brownstone roof, startling a boy and setting off a complicated episode, the effects of which reach far into the future. The maid must clean up Randall's gory mess, a young couple argue over what to do about the recovered note, and on and on through a series of consequences no less real because they don't touch Eugene Randall's fading life in the cozily humanistic way conventional realists teach readers to expect. Instead of answering questions, Dixon's story generates new fictions, as when the boy claims someone has tried to shoot him. "Now what kind of story is that?" (p. 2) a neighbor asks, as this new thread of narrative spins itself out, among many others, from Eugene Randall's terminal act.

"14 Stories" is a good example of how Dixon avoids the facile signaling of conventional realism in favor of the richer possibilities of signs at play. Makes of autos, tastes in music, styles and qualities of clothing—all these are bits and pieces of the real world which realists use to signal a certain type of character or development of plot. They locate the reader in an identifiable world and serve as a shorthand notation of attitudes and values the author wishes employed. There is always the danger that fiction might become sociology when these signals take over and become the work itself; in any event, they allow the writer to escape working with his or her fiction, falling back instead on the catalogue of social mores the reader already knows.

Dixon's talent is to stick it out with his materials, to write fiction with them rather than to signal predetermined attitudes, and so he never lets his signifiers rush off into the world in search of the things they represent. Eugene Randall's suicide in a shabby hotel room could easily start a movie running in our heads, but then Dixon's story would be out of control, happening somewhere off the page. Thus the reader is given no more than one line of it before the chambermaid downstairs is seen worrying about the sound, and no more than a moment of that before an equally interesting narrative begins about the kid up the block who has been nearly nicked by the shot. With such rapid shifts there is no time to lose oneself in the illusion of story, for another one is ready to begin; soon the play of signs becomes a self-conscious act in itself. From sentence to sentence there is a great deal of writing to be done before anyone can sit back and say they know it all.

Unlike the conventional realists who pretend the world is an easy place to have and hold, Dixon knows that things go on. At least six distinct actions take place in the title story, more if every new involvement is counted. Moreover, with each little tale there is an endless regression of fact. For example, the boy's neighbor never should have touched the bullet before calling the police. "If I'd been smart I should have let him pass when he came flying downstairs," the man admits. "I never should have left my flat for cigarettes—never should have been smoking, in fact. Cancer I'll get, and also a jail sentence. In fact, I never should have taken my first puff when I was young and everyone said don't take your first puff, Willy, because it will lead to bad things. Little did they know. Do you smoke, Warren?" (p. 8) he asks the boy, and we are back to the first level of narration, ready for more. There is no end to it, as the true genius of signs knows:

the world goes on and on, and to section off any part of it is an act of artistic fraudulence.

So many simultaneous interests might be a strategy prompted by the short attention spans and precipitous boredom of contemporary audiences, but this habit of stretching things to their full extent and beyond runs through all of Stephen Dixon's work and serves a deeper purpose. In "Mac in Love" from his first collection, *No Relief*,[12] the narrator's girlfriend is breaking off their affair (a perennial Dixon theme), and under these conditions nothing is simple, as the story's techniques show. A nice day? Yes, blue sky, but there is pollution which the eye cannot see "because of something to do with particles and refraction" (p. 8) and on and on while the relationship, tenuous even in its better days, is sustained now only by language. Even on his way out the door there are conversations which by virtue of words and syntax can be stretched to infinity, just as the repercussions from Eugene Randall's bullet generated any number of succeeding texts. Consider this final variation on a sentence which has grown through the preceding paragraphs: "Will you please thank Ruth for telling Mrs. Roy to tell Ruth to tell you to tell Mrs. Roy to tell Ruth to tell you your watering can's on the window ledge?" (p. 17). Robbe-Grillet's phenomenological realism is capable of laborious description, but never with such comedy behind it— and never with language's own action, rather than the object's, as its substance.

In Dixon's work a five-hundred word sentence is not unusual, though its variety of combinational techniques rarely makes it boring to read. What begins as an attempt to capture it all, as in the seemingly realistic sketch of a narrator's comatose father dying in a hospital, ends as a virtual recreation of the old man's helpless state. Simple instructions for communication—blink once if you hear me, twice if you don't—soon extend themselves to the ridiculous even as they try harder and harder, through qualification after qualification, to succeed. The hallmark of this behavior, and of this style, is persistence. Both Dixon's narrators and his sentences go on and on, until credibility turns incredible and then back into the believable again. Mac keeps saying good-bye until the police warn him, and then again as they carry him off. Another narrator annoys a woman in a cafeteria through all manner of brush-offs, rejections, threats, physical violence, and mayhem. In Stephen Dixon's work there is no simple end to anything, as if the conventions of realism are a Pandora's box which, once opened, must be faithfully and persistently explored.

The novels are built on similar situations, and their plots show that Dixon's way of writing sentences and setting scenes works for full-length plots as well. *Work*[13] is a testimony both to the dogged persistence it takes to find a job and the ridiculous lengths to which one must go to hold it. Hunting one down takes the narrator one-third of the book, and that is the easy part. Once employed as a bartender in a restaurant chain he has to cope with a self-contained universe of rules and relationships: how to mix drinks, charge for specials, move traffic, scan papers for bar talk news, spot company spies, handle rush hour jams, deal with the company union, foil stick-ups, soothe tempers, counsel neurot-ics, and keep this whole wacky symphony of waiters, dishwash-ers, assistant managers, cashiers, and customers in line. And this is just three or four pages into the action. Rather than sig-nals of social attitudes, these are the devices which generate Dix-on's text, keeping it going with such vigor and gusto that one day's work shift provides enough excitement to fill a chapter.

Dixon's second novel, *Too Late*,[14] takes his two favorite top-ics—breaking off a relationship and suffering complications which run on *ad infinitum*—and rushes them through a breathless ex-perience in the urban jungle, during which four days pass like four minutes of excitement or four centuries of deliberate tor-ture. The narrator's girlfriend leaves him in a movie, the vio-lence of which has sickened her. But she never makes it home. The film's brutality has set the stage for the narrator to imagine the worst: where is she, and why? The police want to treat it as a brush-off, but the narrator resists this suggestion (as always) and is seduced by the textual universe of other possibilities, of signs and signals run amok: abduction, rape, murder, or worse. The very worst that a frightened person can imagine is just what transpires. Kooks and crazies who feed on news sensationalism rush into the narrator's life, and he himself goes through a Jekyll-and-Hyde transformation of losing his job, annoying friends, bothering neighbors, tearing up his apartment, forging a ransom note (to motivate the police), and running off helter-skelter after the shadiest of clues to his lover's whereabouts. *Too Late* is structured as a tangled web of disruptions and distractions, of realistic conventions which are allowed to run off out of control; they are the very stuff of Dixon's fiction which is in this novel shown to be an ever-present possibility of city life.

The question which occupies the center of Dixon's work—the fragility of human relationships, compounded by the danger of reality running off into infinite digressions and qualifications as stability collapses—is answered by the book which synthesizes his talents as a short fictionist and novelist: the integrated collection, *Quite Contrary: The Mary and Newt Story*.[15] These eleven fictions treat the three-year, off-and-on affair of a couple the likes of which run through nearly all of Dixon's writing. Such involvements, he says, include endless complications; love begets much more than love in return. Their first meeting and the start of their relationship, for example, are based on parting:

> "I don't know. I don't like the roles. You asking. Why couldn't I have asked you? Because again, I don't want to. Why not whatever we might do only when and if we feel like it? Let's start by leaving here. Do you want to?"
>
> "Yes I do."
>
> "Me too. Then if out front we still want to walk together, okay. And if not, or even going downstairs we want to part, then we do. If we don't want to part on the stairs or in front of the building, and a block away, let's say, we still want to be together, then we will. And on and on like that till either of us doesn't want to be with the other person or both of us don't want to stop. Well, sometimes in the future one of us will want to stop, but not until that person says so, okay?" (Pp. 71–72)

Dixon's couples are a fated mismatch: he is "too demanding," she has just departed one marriage and doesn't want to be tied down again too soon. Their tendency to break up is in fact the cement of their relationship. If Newt tries to tell a friend that he and Mary are "this time really through," he faces the reply: "Nah, you two are never really through. You're a pair: Tom and Jerry, Biff and Bang. You just tell yourselves you're through to make your sex better and your lives more mythic and poetic and to repeatedly renew those first two beatific weeks you went through" (p. 19).

Like the parting scene in "Mac in Love," these particular qualities of the Mary and Newt story lend themselves to articulation—endless articulation—and what otherwise in a relationship might not even be noticed is here endlessly explained. Self-effacing realism would miss these elements, since they are the stuff of language rather than of event. Conversely, a less linguistically self-apparent affair might be over and done with before much fiction could be made from it; it is unlikely a conventional realist would ever tell the couple's story, since so much of it depends upon their self-apparent words which Dixon's techniques profile. Mary and Newt's experience is sustained by language and therefore kept before our imaginative attention.

The story-collection form of *Quite Contrary* lets Dixon use form as well as content to accomplish his narration, and here we see how his views of human relationship and the quality of reality which self-apparent fiction catches are one and the same. Mary and Newt's rocky affair provides material for storytelling, but also hints for different ways to structure their tale. Indeed, the telling is the story. "Man of Letters" prints sixteen drafts of a single break-up letter which concludes with the decision not to split up at all—a choice encouraged by the textuality of the narrator's own writing, an example of how technique can become its own substance and sustenance. "The Meeting" tries to explain the odd circumstances of a relationship which began with a sustained parting. Under the gun of explaining such odd behavior the narrator finds he cannot tell a straight story and so pleads: "Let me start again, though keeping my confusion in. I don't know why, but right now that seems important to me." If his writing effaces itself, the special point of the relationship will be lost, and so instead he opts for self-apparency, "To involve the reader in the actual writing act" (p. 60). This self-questioning continues throughout the story and makes its own point, which the puzzling content alone might have obscured. "Em" and "Mary's Piece" are the two narrators' attempts to make sense of one another, and *making sense* is defined as a writing problem (they even discuss submitting these very stories to magazines). "The Franklin Stove" begins with the narrator off at a writers' colony, composing a Mary and Newt break-up story; it ends back in his apartment with Mary herself seducing him away from his typewriter—and away from his apparent intention to leave. When the affair does reach its finish (as finally as possible, for the book itself is coming to a close, with only ten pages left) the writer presents an aptly named "Prolog" in which his grief is so massive and disruptive that it can no longer be screamed, spoken, or even typed, "so I type goodnight" (p. 200).

From *No Relief* and *Quite Contrary* Dixon has proceeded with collections which cohere without any formal theme except the exercise of technique, which in itself proves to be as interesting as the illusion of story. The true synthesis for any self-apparent writer is finally on the level of form. Among the pieces collected in *14 Stories*, an old man dying in a hospital ("Cut") is the focus of a dozen different actions, including those of relatives, visitors, doctors, nurses, orderlies, and so on, not to mention his own concerns. Shifting point of view from paragraph to paragraph thus tells the same story and many different stories all at once; the most common of realistic techniques is here used self-apparently to show how many different realities compete around this pitifully wasted man who cannot exert his own dominance. Speech and dialogue, two more simple parts of realism, yield marvelously transformative effects simply by having their consonants juggled, as in the otherwise pornographic story "Milk

Is Very Good For You" which becomes a slapstick farce: "We were in red, Jane heated on top of me, my sock deep in her funt and linger up her masspole . . . " (p. 26); the normal turn of events is further thrown off center by having the characters express insatiable desires for milk. A simple event, such as a whirlwind romance and just as sudden breakup, is told again and again with the winds of love and disaffection whirling faster each time ("Love Has Its Own Action"); writing this way soon changes reality into absurd improbability, though each step has been small enough so that one never knows just where common sense turns crazy.

How stories need reshaping (for truthfulness of effect) is demonstrated by Dixon's fourth collection, *Movies*.[16] The title piece shows how the substance of a popular film has less effect than its interpretation, and that all interpretations are different, to the point of human relationships foundering in their wake. "The Watch" combines several Dixon techniques to create a situation in which the narrator gives a panhandler his pocket watch by mistake, and must then argue with the bum, a gathering crowd, and the police as he tries to clarify the situation. In "The Barbecue" a party guest tries to tell the company a story, but only their promptings for changes and embellishments allows him to finally get it "right." When a bear wanders across a cottage site in Maine, a man and wife have great trouble reporting the incident to each other, let alone to the game warden and other authorities, and when a newspaper story appears the next day, the facts are changed once again ("Small Bear"). The most amusing story of this group is "The Moviemaker," in which a writer publishes his novel about his breaking up with an old lover only to have her phone him with demands that she adapt it for the movies. Her script will contain numerous revisions, with persons, places, and things altered to fit the image she had tried to project in their relationship. As before with real life, the narrator now resists her tampering with his story. She counters with the taunt that he will probably concoct a salable short story from her present phone call—as he obviously has to judge from the piece of fiction being read. These techniques are not reflexive or metafictional, for something "real" is taking place in each. Yet those elements of reality are conventionally self-apparent, for the reader is urged to take part in the compositional nature of each event, no part of which may be taken for granted. The affairs of life are dangerously unstable, and reporting them is even more volatile a business than trying to live them, as Dixon's besieged lover/narrators learn at every turn.

The other self-apparent principle *Movies* demonstrates is how fictions are generated. In earlier stories by Dixon whimsy was often the structural basis for affairs, romantic or bureaucratic, which went on and on according to their own ludic possibilities. In this collection "The Shirt" recalls the playful style: the narrator is given an ill-fitting, uncomfortable shirt by a well-meaning neighbor, and for page after page endures an ever-complicating series of events (involving inputs of everyone else's trouble) as he tries to give the shirt away. New for Dixon are stories which accommodate this structure to less comic circumstances. In "Cy" a disfigured narrator undergoes an unending series of humiliations and inflictions of cruelty, each more unspeakable and inhumane than the last, as if to test both the writer's genius and the reader's patience at enduring such unpleasantness. "Darling" begins with the polite, courteous, and loving exchanges between a bedridden invalid and the narrator who is hired to care for her. But within this gentle rhythm Dixon soon inserts incidents of wanton cruelty, which escalate until the narrator is unleashing virtual mayhem upon his helpless victim (he finally burns the house down). The collection's most deft use of the generating principle, however, is in the concluding piece, "The Frame." Here the narrator is visiting a shop to have a picture framed. The clerk is a handicapped woman whose affliction reminds him of his late sister's disability. What begins as a casual conversation on this subject—interspersed, of course, with the typical Dixon busyness with the fuss and bother of getting the right frame ordered—soon surrenders its focus to a second story of the sister herself dying in a hospital, attended by the narrator and other family members. For a time the two stories alternate, but at the crucial concluding moment they merge, with the narrator glancing at another customer as he leaves the store and suddenly seeing the elevator door open and his mother arrive outside his dead sister's room.

Love and Will[17] returns Dixon to his more familiarly humorous appraisals of life, only here the humor extends from content to structure. In "The Rehearsal," for example, the narrator courts an opera singer from afar as she rehearses an open-air concert in the Central Park band shell. They meet and arrange a date, but only on the last of twenty pages, the nineteen previous having been devoted to his preparation for their meeting. "Heat" helps explain Dixon's fascination with the internal gears of bureaucracy which are a perfect model for the generating principles of short stories (which also have only their own existence to justify their reason for being). For the story's length the narrator fights with his landlord and the city to get some heat to his freezing apartment building; but at the story's end, with the heat finally restored, his quizzing of the building inspector as to how he and the other tenants can avoid such problems in the future is answered by the inspector's own question as to where the next address on his complaint sheet may be found—ultimate solutions to such problems cannot be found if the system is to be maintained.

Such an appreciation of what the stuff of life is gives *Love and Will* its sense of vital humanity. From its repetitious heartbeat, life goes on by virtue of its routine, but that very routine can generate the conflicts which tear people apart, as in the story "The Argument," which has begun with one partner leaving a room because the other has entered it.

Now we're still discussing things in a relatively unquarrelsome manner. But you want to know why we're about to get into another bad argument? Because you insist on doing something you know is impossible for me to allow you to do without our getting into another bad argument, which is the main reason we got into the last bad argument that led up to all this. Now please, for both of us, turn around and go into one of the other rooms or outside or anyplace else, but leave me alone in this room. (P. 157)

"Tails" suggests how this seemingly organic nature to quarrel and debate is built into the structure of human relationships, thanks to the nature of language, which as Wittgenstein pointed out is at the root of all philosophical problems.

"I'm cold. You must be cold. Let me feel your lips. Usually your lips are cold if it's cold out. Your lips are cold. Very cold. So it must be cold out. Very cold. I like cold. I'm going out." She goes out. (P. 186)

Life is problematic, Dixon shows, in both its experience and depiction, because both are functions of language. And language, despite its reluctance for self-apparency, is the commerce of fiction. The type of honesty both life and fiction demand creates a realism one can never take for granted. Knowing the world—and all that can happen in it—is an epistemological adventure, and it is Stephen Dixon's achievement that familiar techniques can be used for such a unique process of reading. There are no "conventions" in his stories, for everything is happening quite literally for the very first time. The stories of *Time to Go*[18] bear out this sense of reality's novelty. "The Bench" begins with an affectionate portrait of a new father bouncing his baby on his knee for all to observe in a public park. But after several weeks both he and the baby disappear, and everyone who has seen them has a different story to account for their absence. And once the man himself reappears, minus baby, he is ready to disavow ever being there in the first place. But a half dozen stories have been generated by the experience, which justifies the production of Dixon's text. In "Meeting Aline" the narrator finds his own experience segmented into three distinct levels: dreaming of an encounter with an old lover, meeting her by chance in a public square, and preparing himself for the inevitable reintroduction. "Don," one of Dixon's longest stories (8,000 words as compared to his customary 2,500), is a cubist narrative of disjunctive paragraphs, each giving a single incident in the protagonist's life linked by only the most superficial of associations; again, the difference in levels of experience produces a distortion when thrown so closely into line.

The title story of this most recent collection shows Dixon at his fullest as a self-apparent master of technique. "Time to Go" takes the familiar circumstance of a father's lingering influence over his son and, through the convention of dialogue, projects it as a real object in itself, despite the fact that it is plausibly impossible. What would otherwise be two narrative tracks, the realistic and the fantastic, are here melded, as the long-dead father accompanies his son to buy an engagement gift for a young woman of whom the old man disapproves. Next time out it is to buy wedding bands, and as the young couple are fitted the father's presence makes itself felt, not as reminiscence or superstition but as an integral part of the story's narrative.

"Something very simple," I say.

He holds up his ring finger. "Nothing more simple and comfortable than this one. I've been wearing it without taking it off once for forty-five years."

"That's amazing," Magna says. "Not once?"

"I can't. I've gained sixty pounds since I got married and my finger's grown around it. Maybe he'll have better luck with his weight. He's so slim now, he probably will."

"More patter," my father says. "Then when you're off-guard they knock you over the head with the price. But remember: this is the Diamond Center. The bargaining's built into the price. Here they think it's almost a crime not to, so this time whatever price he quotes, cut him in half."

"Single or double-ring ceremony?" Nat asks.

"Double," Magna says, "and identical rings."

"Better yet," my father says. "For two rings you have even greater bargaining power. Cut him more than half." [19]

When the son resists, his father chides; when Magna adopts his line of reasoning, he cheers her on. The fact that he never speaks to her nor takes part in their conversations is hardly noticed, so dominant is his presence within his son's memory—and it is that memory, and not external credibility of action, which establishes the textual plane of the story. When at last the son adopts his father's standards of value and begins exercising them, the father fades into the background, confident that the story's form will do the job. At the end, celebrating his son's wedding, he is embraced . . . and disappears.

By their privileging of the writer and his techniques over the action he represents, Walter Abish and Stephen Dixon have saved fiction from the sterile abstractions of reflexivity and metafiction, restoring instead the full human sense of which writing is meant to impart. The work of Clarence Major continues in this direction, but pointing even more so at the text itself which draws its sense of human life from the apparency of its construction. His novel *Reflex and Bone Structure*[20] reveals its own compositional integrity on every page, yet still manages to tell a story replete with human fascination. As Tzvetan Todorov has remarked, of all fictive subgenres it is the detective novel which "tends toward a purely geometric architecture,"[21] and so Major chooses that form for his first experiment with self-apparency. In detective fiction the subject matter of the plot has been concluded before the novel begins: the crime is an established fact, and now the author and reader must concentrate on its solution. In other words, the novel must compose itself not around the unfolding of a represented story but rather with the more epistemological business of sorting things out—mediating, as it were, between the a priori fact and the reader's appreciation of it. The text therefore assumes a reality of its own, as the reader's relationship to the author takes on the deeply realistic qualities of the detective's posture toward the crime. Narrative action is not something reported or even reflected; it is the existence of the book itself.

Yet *Reflex and Bone Structure* is more than a conventional detective novel, for every element of its composition—character, theme, action, and event—expresses the self-apparent nature of its making. Characterization is done through metaphors, emphasizing artifice to the point of allegory. Even events take on this supra-real quality.

> We're all at a party suddenly. Place full of cranks dumbbells failures showoffs playgirls juveniles boozers fallen-angels chatterboxes twotime losers meanies snobs, you name it. Canada is drinking a lot and Cora is beginning to flirt. She's in a musty hallway with someone. Dale is in the toilet letting his horse out to pasture. Cora wants to go play pony express with somebody. I smile, they smile. (P. 1)

Two pages and another party later, the scene is even more bizarre, with "healthy cows and chickens . . . standing around the living room, mooing and clucking." Is this simply a case of hallucination or overly poetic perception? Yes, but in a way which Major demonstrates to be within the fictional quality of all life.

> It's too much. I take Cora home in a taxi.
> We're in bed watching the late movie. It's 1938. *A Slight Case of Murder*. Edward G. Robinson and Jane Bryan.
> I go into the bathroom to pee. Finished, I look at my aging face. Little Caesar. I wink at him in the mirror. He winks back.
> I'm back in bed. The late show comes on. It's 1923. *The Bright Shawl*. Dorothy Gish. Mary Astor. I'm taking Mary Astor home in a yellow taxi. Dorothy Gish is jealous. (P. 3)

Here the effect is more than commonly poetic or hallucinogenic, for in the simple reality of watching television one becomes transposed to the time and space on the screen: in a 1938 movie it *is* 1938. Identifying vicariously with characters is only an extension of this basic fact. At other times Major's narrators talk of the transforming power of music, how listening to a record effectively changes one's reality, both emotional and actual. To emphasize this condition he never describes a character playing records but instead says, "*The Jimi Hendrix Experience* jumps through the room with the force of Goya dancers" (p. 22) or, even more transformationally, "Canada has to find a way to relax. He sends for Red Garland to play piano. . . . Stan Getz follows Red. . . . He's back in 1938 listening to Ella sing, 'A-tisket,

A-tasket"' (p. 52). Other times, "to keep my mind off the problem of Cora's death," the narrator watches television, because "in the afternoon TV is dull shit and it lodges you in its dullness; yet it gives you a weird vegetable sort of copout security" (p. 36). And again, "He turned on the television and the world seemed normal as all get out" (p. 95).

Every element within Major's narrative is animated, sometimes by the characters and other times by the narrator himself. "Cora was not afraid of her own unconscious life," we're told. "She believed in the interplay between it and what she saw and felt everyday. Like Canada's dick. Or his face. Or the pots and pans. Or the stove and the kitchen table or the butcher knife which, sometimes, she felt like running through Canada's back" (p. 33). Cora's rural southern past is also a concrete reality, as the narrator notes salamanders, tree frogs, and other native fauna nestling amid the clutter of her New York apartment. Anthropologically speaking, there is no simple reality in this novel, only a plethora of cultural descriptions all competing for persuasive presence. An actress on television is never just that; there is the role she's playing, the physical conditions of the production within which she works, plus the equally real life she may be living at that very moment in her apartment across town. Television, music, fantasies, and history—all conspire to create a larger reality which Major's writings dutifully embrace.

> Canada comes home and finds the rubber plant doing the dishes. Cora is reading a book about Jerome Kern.
> A blind snake is curled in the middle of the floor.
> Rita Hayworth is screaming in the room. Canada looks around. Oh. The television.
> Later that night, Canada does a transatlantic lindy hop from Europe to the states and landing in a courtroom in the South, he accidentally gets sentenced to the penitentiary as one of the Scottsboro boys. (P. 46)

Within the narrative of the crime's detection (Cora has been murdered), Major treats us to the characters' own projective fantasies. Cora has her own dream of an elegant house in the country, filled with *chic* ideas from *Better Homes & Gardens* and *Elle*, and like a novelist she tries to construct little dramas within it.

> Often Cora tries to invest Dale with her own vision of the house, with herself in it, in the kitchen. She sees herself standing at the sink with an apron tied around her naked body and Dale approaching her from behind. He has just come home from his job where he is happy, where he is boss. No. That's Dale's vision. Cora erases it and replaces it with her own: she's at the sink, but she's fully dressed. In fact she's wearing a long, elegant, cardigan evening gown that clings to her lovely figure. (P. 41)

The narrator is prone to these same fantasies as well; indeed, the characters' fiction-making is simply a microcosmic example of his own activity in creating this novel. Therefore he marshals these emotions to help construct *Reflex and Bone Structure*. His own feelings for Cora are ravaged by the jealousy he feels when pairing her with the other two males, Canada and Dale. His imagination sometimes runs to violence, picturing his characters in airplane crashes or explosions—as well he might, for he is after all writing the novel and enjoys a God-like power over his creations. Most importantly, he has his own voice in this fiction, convincing to the reader because it reveals his fully human plight in dealing with the emotions at hand.

> I'll take the gun into the front room and threaten to kill them both if they don't stop laughing. I will tell them that, and if they don't stop, I'll really do it. I think I'll do it. I hope I *can* do it. I don't really know if I should do it but, perhaps, if I start by lifting the weapon and walking away toward the front with it in my hand, the reason for doing it might suddenly develop. Right now, I know no reason. I have no reason. My thoughts are the kind people keep to themselves. Like the fear of dying and everybody's endless quiet desperation. (P. 38)

On a more specific level, the narrator identifies problems he is having with his characters. Cora comes easily, for she is his obsession. Canada he respects, partly because this figure can wield the violent impulses which the narrator can only express in writing. But Dale, the necessary third point of this triangle, presents a problem. Throughout the 145 pages of this brief novel there are no less than seven references to this dilemma. "I have almost no sense of Dale except I know I don't like him" (p. 11), we are told, and soon the narrator sends him out to North Dakota so he can have some creative rest. "The fact that Dale really has little or no character doesn't help matters," he complains. "I cannot help him if he refuses to focus." There is even a bit of jealousy here, for "whatever it was about him that attracted Cora shall always remain a mystery to me" (p. 42). There is a temptation to punish this character, to run him through a series of embarrassing episodes, but in the end the narrator admits the key to the problem. "Dale was never meant to make it. He was that side of myself that should be rewritten. Dale was an argument I had with the past" (p. 144). Here once more a temptation of the life-seeking reader—that characters are projections of different facets of the author's own personality—is turned around to become a self-apparent component in the work itself.

Cora is indeed the narrator's obsession, and the male figures—Canada and Dale—have been the respectively positive and negative aspects of his own mania which blossom forth into fiction. The only unconventional aspect of all this has been Major's willingness to let the reader see behind the scenes and to incorporate this perspective into the making of his novel. There are many ways to approach Cora. "Canada tries too hard some times," we're told at the beginning. "He tries to crack into Cora. Burst into Cora. Open Cora with his sledge-hammer. But I weave *around* the stern cathedrals in her holy city, her very pure spirit" (p. 2). A world war can erupt over a person as a sex object, Major recalls, alluding to Troy and subsequent human disasters: *Reflex and Bone Structure* is an attempt to locate this energy within one narrator and show how it can create a novel just as well.

Throughout the novel Major makes integral references to the work at hand. "It's snowing outside. I'm in here making this novel" (p. 51) is typical, as is the resigned complaint, two-thirds of the way through, that "when I have to deal with Cora I'm forced to think too much. I'd rather drink beer with Cora and not try to untangle the mystery of her presence and her dreams of swollen food. Couldn't be anything but sex" (p. 87). Major's travails as author are much like the fictive-making agonies of his characters within their various jealousies, fantasies, and paranoid reactions; because he establishes the identities among these acts and the correlative reality between his feelings and his characters', *Reflex* becomes a meaningful text for the reader—both as an adventure of its characters and of its author. Having alerted his readers to what's happening, Major can move his perception from character to character as the mood demands, so that "I'm never alone. It is either Canada or Cora and sometimes Dale" (p. 89). At times they can become fictionists as well, as Canada "invents and reinvents the world as he wishes it to be" (p. 31). What is real for a character is just as real for the author, and vice versa; the text of *Reflex and Bone Structure* is essentially one thing, added to the world, rather than a representation of any one part.

At the heart of it all is the narrator's obsession with Cora. "I close my eyes and she walks inside my skull" (p. 111). "Parts of her did however get into print" (p. 113) in Major's earlier novels, but here she controls the work entirely, being created (for after all, the real Cora is dead) by the words. "I'm extending reality," the narrator insists, "not retelling it" (p. 49). The novel becomes his infatuation, his seduction, his recreation of her. "Writing words on paper has a powerful effect on his mind" (p. 83), for sure, because this way Cora is brought to life once more. "Please person be Cora. Just this once be Cora. You are Cora person. Please" (p. 93). Once vitalized, Major can do what Beckett requested of Joyce, that his fictions not be about something but rather be something themselves.

> Get to this: Cora isn't based on anybody.
> Dale isn't anything.
> Canada is just something I'm busy making up.

> I am only an act of my own imagination. I cannot even hear my
> own voice the way they hear it. I got the "Bullfrog Blues."
> Cora does the "Charleston Rag."
> Dale sings "Hello Dolly."
> Canada covers the waterfront. (P. 85)

Above all, as in a detective novel, the final truth is less important than the process of getting to it in its full implications. And
as in the process of detection, the author's activity is prominent.

> And by being alone so much reinforces the tendency to skin-dive
> beneath the surface. Not that I find solutions. I should ideally strike
> a balance between the surface and the lower depths. I can do the
> low stuff very effectively. I need practice on the surface where Cora,
> Canada and Dale hang out. (P. 96)

There is never any illusion, for "everything Cora does happens
first in my mind" (p. 140).

That happening is essentially a work of linguistic craftsman-
ship, and just as Cora's existence is sparked by her name on the
page (as writing a loved one's name is a familiar emotional resort
in conjuring a presence), so, too, does that constructive act remind the reader that all is essentially invented. When Cora sleeps,
the word *sleep* sleeps with her, so vitalistic has the author's language become. What happens in life is secondary to what happens in this novel: such is the transformative power of language,
reversing the general trend of conventionally representative fiction. For after all, this is a detective novel, and according to the
genre's rules there is, on the story level, no hope for Cora—she
is dead and gone before the action begins. That action, however,
is an attempt to figure out the crime and also to will Cora back
into life, such is the author's emotional obsession with her.
Therefore the words on the page are more real than any imagined
picture of the factually now-dead woman.

> I am standing behind Cora. She is wearing a thin black night-
> gown. The backs of her legs are lovely. I love her. The word stand-
> ing allows me to watch like this. The word nightgown is what she

is wearing. The nightgown itself is in her drawer with her panties. The word Cora is wearing the word nightgown. I watch the sentence: The backs of her legs are lovely. (P. 74)

Major's paragraph lets us read his sentence two ways: either representationally, that "the backs of her legs are lovely," or—in full knowledge of the fact that she is dead and only the novelist's words are conjuring up her presence—that the sentence itself creates her. To any reader, these same words mean much more the second time through.

Emergency Exit[22] is an even fuller work, just as any novel per se eclipses the effect of a subgenre in the end. In it Major focuses on every componential level of writing as a thing in itself, creating a virtual catalogue of self-apparent effects in fiction. Superintending the whole is an anthropological device around which the novel's action is based: the institution of a "threshold law" which requires all the women of a modern American town to be carried across doorways, a symbolic act based upon ancient tribal taboos regarding menstruation. "Stop: The doorway of life," Major's novel begins, and then immediately takes "this cliché" and revitalizes the dead metaphor with meaning. As Wittgenstein would suggest, it is all a problem with language, here expressed as a "male attitude toward the female" which because of fundamental confusions between signifier and signified leads to a misconstrued symbology.

> Because women are eternally guilty of sin they had to be lifted and carried across the threshold and they could not *touch* the doorway. Yet they, the givers of life itself, were the *source* of the symbolism and the ritual. They were the doorway of life. (P. 1)

A threshold law, then, is an originally transparent signifier which because of faulty syntax has become an opaque sign, a thing in itself, signifying nothing but its own dead language.

Major parallels his own act of writing with *Emergency Exit*'s theme, using each component in fiction, right down to the very words themselves, as opaque objects before incorporating them in the novel's larger syntax. In this manner words, sentences, paragraphs, vignettes, short stories, and the plot line itself are established as things in themselves before taking on their larger referential duties—and even then the reader's attention will be directed not off the page but back to it, where each word was first introduced as an artifact. Following his documentary introduction of the threshold law, complete with a reproduction of the signed city ordinance, he includes a paragraph of pure writing: first describing an actual scene ("The sky cleared. The backyard is beautiful"), then showing how he proceeds to write about it (p. 7). The act is at once representational and artificial, much like Malcolm Morley's "The Last Painting of Vincent Van Gogh" where within a superrealistic frame of landscape, paint box, and easel Van Gogh's own abstractly expressive canvas is shown.

Following this are two hundred and fifty pages of fiction, interpolated with two dozen of Major's own paintings. His styles of writing and art complement each other, each growing from a material emphasis on simple components to the employment of these same devices in eventual figuration. As words and sentences build into paragraphs and emerging plots, so, too, do the starkly primitive black lines on white backgrounds (reminiscent of works by Franz Kline and Robert Motherwell) slowly take shape (circles), form biomorphic images (weirdly allusive heads and torsos, as in paintings by William Baziotes), create dances of energy on the canvas (think of Jackson Pollock, Willem de Kooning, and the push-pull effect of Hans Hofmann), and finally resolve themselves into a figure on page 76: a recognizable image of a woman, but faceless, so that the viewer's attention is directed toward the curving lines of her head, shoulders, skirt, and legs—lines which were first established, in previous paintings, as things in themselves.

"In a novel, the only thing you really have is words," Major emphasized in his interview with John O'Brien. "You begin with words and you end with words. The content exists in our minds.

I don't think that it has to be a reflection of anything. It is a reality that has been created inside of a book."[23] Therefore his strategy in *Emergency Exit* is to emphasize that every device of human interest (which critics of conventional fiction demand) is first of all a problem in language. His elementary notion of "threshold" is explored by studying every dictionary meaning of the word, from *Webster's* to dictionaries of symbols and indices of folklore. We are also given other documents reporting the word's effect on the community: the phone book, card files in the library, and arrests on the police blotter for its violation. As for the novel's action, it is established to be first of all linguistic. Individual sentences are written on the page, apparently leading nowhere, so that the reader's attention is to their writerly art. If the word "lighthouse" is mentioned, we do not know why, and have no interests to pursue other than its syntactic grace in the sentence (poetic images are not the point). Other sentences are included because they are such obvious artifacts: the stock-in-trade lines of conversation, all numbered and lettered; a series of replies to wrong-number phone calls; conversations which blend into exchanges of nonsense words or blanks, each of which can be filled in by the reader's momentum. By page 77, enough will have been revealed about the characters from other sections that free-standing lines can be matched with appropriate characters. Meanwhile, words and sentences are growing into paragraphs, which in turn pop up again as self-apparent references within the occasional three-page plot interludes. Lists of superstitions, for example, first stand as things in themselves—oft-repeated nuances detached from any real application. So when the narrative application does come, several pages later, the reader will recall that rather than any reference to the real world the narrator is employing a self-conscious artifact which was first introduced as an opaque sign.

The plot itself is emphasized as artifice at every turn. As in *Reflex and Bone Structure*, Major makes frequent reference to his act of writing, even "employing gimmicks," and near the end begins an affair with a character whose liaisons have formed an interesting part of the story (and who has certainly been seducing the reader). Characters themselves are described in surreal terms, so that there is little chance to get lost in their verisimilitude; such deliberate violations of reality as "a blue car passes it is filled with Roslyn taking a steambath" (p. 114) and describing others as nine feet tall and weighing four hundred pounds are just the kind of distortions which remind readers that there is an author making it all up. Other times the narrator addresses the words himself, as in this sentence within an otherwise conventionally narrative passage: "Africa might be a place you could dig after all even after Tarzan and white lies. Little white lies. Hello white lies. White lies uneasily on the canvas" (p. 18), moving within syntax and referentiality from adjective to verb and from racial sociology to personal behavior. There is, moreover, a reality to language, such that a change of synonyms creates a new sense, as the narrator reminds us, "They went to Julie's apartment in the city and fucked but they also made love with each other after fucking became a bore" (p. 19).

To forestall any attempt to receive Major's characters as real, yet to place his inventions within an even more sociologically precise category, he mixes in the self-apparent inventiveness of cartoon figures with the more ordinary actions of his plot.

> Meanwhile darkness moved all around the house. The word dark cannot explain just how dark it was how quiet how peaceful. It was a darkness bought with impressive money. Say Money . . . Barbra Streisand owned a house down the block. Dick Tracy lived two blocks over. Dr. Spock ran a clinic five minutes from here. Norman Mailer spent his summers in a house nearby. (P. 20)

Actions can be at once more fully explicated yet fixed as fantasy in the same way.

> Jim is feeling very tense feels he needs a drink he stops in a bar. Humphrey Bogart is there leaning against the bar. Bogart tries to

smile at Jim but his face doesn't quite make it. Bogart lifts his glass to Jim once Jim has a drink in his hand too. Bogart says, "I don't trust bastards who don't drink." Jim says, "I'll drink to that. By the way what's your name?" Before Bogart can answer this perfectly logical question Roslyn rushes into the tavern. She looks frantic but also a little like Lauren Bacall in one of the early movies. Roslyn, not as Bacall would do, grabs Jim's arm and says, "The car's waiting outside—we'd better go, *fast!*" As they leave Bogart waves and shouts, *"Happy sailing"'* (P. 70)

Here the novel's characters act realistically while at the same time the movie stars behave in character, according to the predictable fantasies of their creation: Bogart's half-smile, gestures, and asides. And because there are Hollywood stars acting out stylized versions of our behavior, a gesture like Bacall's can be a handy point of reference. The paragraph's first sentence incorporates another of Major's devices, here borrowed from Ronald Sukenick's novel *Out*: the transcription of sentences (notably the first without punctuation, so that in run-on fashion sentence the action is impelled forward, which is one more way of preventing the reader from getting absorbed within the referential reality of these words.

On at least a dozen occasions Major refers to some ensuing action as "like a soap opera" or a person's behavior as "like a character in naturalistic fiction." Here again the effect is double, using a type of literary-historical shorthand which contributes to plot and characterization while at the same time noting that it is all arbitrary convention. At times Major can be a theorist as well, such as when his narrator remarks: "He could hear her going and coming. The process of her movements was like Gertrude Stein's fiction. She was in the continuous present" (p. 152)—an indication that aesthetics is just as much about life as it is of art. When someone is introduced as "a very realistic girl" (p. 130), theory and practice coalesce, reminding us that choices in fictional theory are finally indices of personal value. It also works the other way, with art interpreting life itself, as in the situation "he was about to go out alone on the lake in a boat like a Hemingway character" (p. 177), surely a reference no well-read person can today escape when their own lives imitate Hemingway's situations. At one point the reader is given a multiple-choice test on just such matters (pp. 128–29), and is later treated to a writers' workshop on the use of setting and event (pp. 145–47). As all self-apparent fiction ultimately must do, *Emergency Exit* summons the full range of the reader's experience to complete the work, conventions being important not only for what they capsulize in fiction but also for the attitudes they bring from real life. It is all artifice, and knowing that yields a fuller reading. During one otherwise normal conversation, the lines of dialogue are numbered to emphasize their materiality. Another time the characters are enrolled in a conference, where a simple listing of their lectures and discussion topics does the job of narrative. The most extreme example comes on page 174, where the local tennis courts are reproduced with the sounds of three tennis games among the characters noted schematically—as two partners rush the net while others play back for lobs, making narrative points about themselves.

Emergency Exit, therefore, demonstrates how the familiar materials of novel-making can be used as things in themselves while still providing all the human interest readers demand. Indeed, self-apparent fiction compliments the reader by providing more to do. Major's novel summarizes in form the history of the last half century of American art, from the building blocks of abstract expressionism through a certain pop iconography (once again, things from real life as themselves) to the experimental techniques of the superrealists. A regard for the material integrity of art's own making has been at the center of these developments, and with *Emergency Exit* we've been shown how they can be as natural for fiction as well. In the face of such work, even realism becomes different, self-apparent in a way that it never was before, just as the radically new superrealism in painting grew from the principles of abstract expressionism. In this way the techniques of Major's fiction enrich the mainstream, creating a style of "experimental realism" in which the simple act of vision becomes not just an integral work of art but an interpretation of our cultural act of seeing as well.

chapter 6 EXPERIMENTAL REALISM

As opposed to reflection and metafiction, which are alienating approaches that leave little room for reform within the conventions of traditional fiction, self-apparency provides an approach to the genre and a collection of techniques by which illusionistic realism can be reinvented. Our century's aesthetic progress has much to do with this; literature does not deal with reality itself, but rather with what a given culture sees as reality—in the nineteenth century surely an approximation of the thing itself, but in our own times an entirely more problematic matter. A typical fiction by Walter Abish, Stephen Dixon, or Clarence Major incorporates within its vision both the new technology in our lives and the equally new modes of perception by which we see. No artist of one hundred and fifty years ago was faced with the plethora of highly polished reflective surfaces such as confront us today on every urban street corner; no Victorian or Belle Epoque artist might suspect that so much of contemporary reality lay on the surface, or that the artistic glance might include more information than real-life perception might ever contain.

That self-apparent fiction can address itself to the problems of realism while still maintaining the anti-illusionistic principles of innovation can be seen by comparing its features, point by point, with the standards insisted upon by reflexive writing. Like abstract expressionist painting, innovative fiction has prided itself in an "all-over" manner; like paint upon the canvas, words on the page are distinguished by their own action. Stephen Dixon's story "Said" does just this, taking the redundant problematics of identifying each line of dialogue and making that very convention not a transparent signifier but rather a self-apparently opaque sign, a true thing in itself.

> He said, she said.
> She left the room, he followed her.
> He said, she said.
> She locked herself in the bathroom, he slammed the door with his fists.
> He said.
> She said nothing.
> He said.
> He slammed the door with his fists, kicked the door bottom.
> She said, he said, she said.
> He batted the door with his shoulder, went into the kitchen, got a screwdriver, returned and started unscrewing the bathroom doornob.
> She said.
> He said nothing, unscrewed the doornob, pulled the doornob out of the door, but the door stayed locked. He threw the doornob against the door, picked it up and threw it down the hall, banged the door with the screwdriver handle, wedged the screwdriver blade between the door and the jamb and tried forcing the door open. The blade broke, the door stayed locked.
> He said, she said, he said.
> He got about 15 feet down the hall and charged at the door.
> She said
> He stopped.
> She said nothing. Then she said, he said, she said, he said.
> He got about 10 feet down the hall this time and charged at the door.[1]

By dropping out the content which can be imagined to precede each pair of "saids," Dixon forgoes artistic centering in favor of an all-over effect—which is, after all, appropriate to the sub-stanceless nature of most marital fights. No one can remember exactly what a lovers' quarrel was about; each has an all-over quality to its experience, to which this style of writing is nicely suited. Not reality itself but *how we perceive it* is what determines this choice of effect.

Antihierarchal is another principle innovative fiction borrowed from action painting. Hierarchies imply a sense of order, and to be effective that sense depends upon a sustained illusion—a taboo for writing which steadfastly refuses to depict something but rather be something in and of itself. "Through the avoidance of a hierarchy that is related to values outside the actual work, language has a choice of becoming what Roland Barthes refers to as a field of action," as Walter Abish describes this same principle's usefulness for self-apparent fiction.[2] Antihierarchal means divesting the perceived sign of its anthropomorphic qualities, and also of the intellectualism which through the mind's inhibiting factors censors out supposedly extraneous information and highlights what it considers centrally important. A somewhat similar practice was followed by Alain Robbe-Grillet and the other makers of the *nouveau roman*, but with the precisely opposite goal: to capture the thing in itself, the pure object now clearly seen through a purified signifier, rather than the absolute opacity of sign to which Abish aspires. But in either case projective anthropomorphism must be banished, which for fiction means using all of the familiar conventions not as indices of attitudes but rather as verbal collages of self-apparent signs—to be valued in and of themselves for their ingenuity of artifice—as in these three introductory paragraphs from Kenneth Gangemi, Howard McCord, and Leonard Michaels.

> Olt knew he would never see a meteor striking an iceberg, a bat falling into snow, or a clown on a nun. He knew he would never go to a party and talk to thunderstorm experts, roller-coaster experts, vampire experts, sailplane experts. He knew that he would never design bear grottos, furnish a time capsule, live in an orange

grove, wade in a vat of mercury, work in the Dead Letter Office, find narwhale tusks on a beach, see a tampax string at the ballet, smell a burning spice warehouse, overhear two call girls talking shop, or attend a meeting of the Junior League.[3]

"The Geography of Ohio"

Ohio lies fifteen thousand feet below sea level in a great rift valley bisecting the western portion of the northeastern corridor. The border with Indiana is considered by some impassible, and by all as rivalled only by lunar structures of yet undetermined origin. A stone dropped from Pennsylvania does not land in Ohio, but in Indiana, the prevailing upward westerlies prohibiting all but a few major airlines from landing anything in Ohio.[4]

"In the Fifties"

In the fifties I learned to drive a car. I was frequently in love. I had more friends than now.

When Khrushchev denounced Stalin my roommate shit blood, turned yellow, and lost most of his hair.

I attended the lectures of the excellent E. B. Burgum until Senator McCarthy ended his tenure. I imagined N. Y. U. would burn. Miserable students, drifting in the halls, looked at one another.

In less than a month, working day and night, I wrote a bad novel.

I went to school: N. Y. U., Michigan, Berkeley—much of the time.

I had witty, giddy conversation, four or five nights a week, in a homosexual bar in Ann Arbor.

I read literary reviews the way people suck candy.

Personal relationships were more important to me than anything else.

I had a fight with a powerful fat man who fell on my face and was immovable.

I had personal relationships with football players, jazz musicians, ass-bandits, nymphomaniacs, non-specialized degenerates, and numerous Jewish premedical students.

I had personal relationships with thirty-five rhesus monkeys in an experiment on monkey addiction to morphine. They knew me as one who shot reeking crap out of cages with a hose.[5]

Traditional realists would accumulate such details as a way of indicating sensibility (the character's, the writer's), and the best way to judge such style would be on the level of absolute transparency. "I know a writer who wished his prose to be transparent so that only the movement and growth of his story would be in evidence," Gilbert Sorrentino writes in *Splendide-Hotel*,[6] but for the experimental realists these descriptive items do just the opposite work. There is no window here, just a self-contained circuit of odd details which do best when read as referring to themselves. The movement is fully interior, from the roommate's shitting blood to the monkey excrement the narrator must flush away, from the personal relationships with old friends to the business with the addicted primates. Gangemi's details in like manner resist narrative effacement; instead, both reader and character are treated to an experimental sense of life itself, undiluted by craft or program. As Philip Stevick has indicated in *Alternative Pleasures*, using the two latter examples, these paragraphs imply no audience and explain nothing.[7] They are not "background" for anything else. Their only meaning is in the assemblage of verbal collage, which the reader must appreciate for the integrity of its compositional elements. Above all there is no explaining, no meaning, no *world-making*, as Stevick says; these descriptions simply mean themselves. And as themselves, they are delightfully funny and inventive, so different from the thing-making of the *nouveau roman*, which Donald Barthelme regretted as "leaden, self-conscious in the wrong way." The joy of self-apparent signs is their lack of hierarchy and informed meaning, which allows the reader to experience them with a full sense of their own being.

Complementing the antihierarchal quality of signs so used are their properties of hardness and flatness. In order to mean itself, innovative fiction refused to let itself be penetrated. Not a window on the world but a surface on which to act, this style of writing distinguished itself by the hardness of its surface. The experimental realists know that the materials of their fictions are signs, not what the signs represent, and so to direct the reader's attention to this opaque surface writers such as Abish and Dixon have emphasized the sign's material qualities. "Each sign has two halves," Gilles Deleuze observes: "it *designates* an object, it *signifies* something different."[8] That something different is often itself, and learning how to move in society is often an education in learning to read signs for themselves; quite often someone is behaving not as an educated and sensitive person but *as the sign* of just such a being. As Deleuze notes in a scene drawn from Proust,

> Nothing funny is said at the Verdurins, and Mme. Verdurin does not laugh; but Cottard makes a sign that he is saying something funny, Mme. Verdurin makes a sign that she is laughing, and her sign is so perfectly emitted that M. Verdurin, not to be outdone, seeks in his turn for an appropriate mimicry. (P. 6)

Stephen Dixon, whose story of "saids" demonstrates the allover quality of experimental realism, also shows a mastery of other conventions in and for themselves, to the point that he can construct entire stories upon the materiality of signs which for other writers would only be transfer points toward larger meaning. "Mac in Love" sacrifices even the movement of "Said" so that a line of dialogue can slowly expand to become the whole story, as noted in chapter five. Dixon's lovers are forever parting, always coming back to this point—just like the sentence in "Mac in Love." The breakups, of course, must be signaled by conventions of dialogue or behavior, and so it is this act of signification which lends a truly textual sense to their affair. In a typical Dixon story plots will go on forever, weaving themselves in a self-apparency of material to the extent that the reader can only take pleasure from the process itself, for any attempt to see through the signifiers to some ultimate meaning is quickly frustrated.

Action painting was complemented by color field painting, and experimental realism has been able to adopt each principle with ease and notable success. Placing minimally imperative language within a floating field of stylization is how writing can achieve this effect. Malcolm Bradbury's novel in progress, *Rates of Exchange*, is essentially situational (like a color field canvas): an introduction to an imaginary eastern European country, where the British protagonist's visit is described within the greater language-scape of the *Guide Michelin*. In the opening chapter nearly all attention is given to the country—its history, customs, sights, tariffs, and regulations. But always there is a deft reference to the traveler who *will visit*; this syntactic imperative is the linguistic field within which the visitor is seen, making him quite a different person than he might have been when departing Heathrow or Gatwick. His subsequent behavior is always within a language which calls attention to itself, the field of the *Baedeker* or *Guide Bleu*. These are the only type of book written with such peculiar linguistic posture, and to have the comic adventures of a British writer take place within their shape is a constant reminder of the novel's self-apparency.

Most crucially, a story's action must take place on the linguistic surface. Although other effects, such as materiality and field, can be applied analogically, the linguistic surface of behavior is at once central to both fictive theory (from Wittgenstein and Saussure to Derrida and Kristeva) and practice. "This is a familiar world," Walter Abish begins a novella.

> It is a world crowded with familiar faces and events. Thanks to language the brain can digest, piece by piece, what has occurred and what may yet occur. It is never at a loss for the word that signifies what is happening this instant. In Mrs. Ite's brain the interior of her large house with a view of the garden and the lake are surfaces of the familiar. She is slim, and moves quite gracefully from one familiar interior to the next. Her movements are impelled by familiar needs.[9]

The novella's plot follows from this same theory, that human needs are shaped by the surfaces of what is available—in this case, by language. A French filmmaker has come to America to

see how a new shopping mall fits this structure. Abish, trained
and once employed as a city planner, sees that the three levels of
activity—mall building, filmmaking, and language—are all
predicated on the availability of surface (urban topography and
economic life, the celluloid strip, the generative syntax), and his
novella works its way out in just the same manner as his more
obviously and mechanically disciplined novel, *Alphabetical Africa*. What he has said of that novel applies to "This Is Not A
Film" as well. "I was fascinated to discover the extent to which
a system could impose upon the contents of a work meaning
which was fashioned by the form, and then to see the degree to
which the form, because of the conspicuous obstacles, under-
mined that very meaning." [10] The characters in his story delight
in life upon the surface; Ping-Pong is a favorite sport, and one
person (the table tennis champ) loves to operate his forklift truck
at work, rearranging cases of soda pop on an asphalt parking lot.
The shopping mall itself creates a topology of need, the syntax
within which Abish's people will cheerfully generate their sentences and plot out their lives.

Abish's most complete work of experimental realism is his
novel *How German Is It*, [11] winner of the first Faulkner/PEN Award
for Fiction in 1981. Here there are no obvious devices such as
the alphabet or linguistic proscription. Instead, like a superreal-
ist painter, Abish has sought out circumstances from real life
which confirm our culture's unique patterns of sight, feeling,
and thought. As a result, the quality of "life" in *How German Is
It* is just as apparently artificial as in one of Ralph Goings' California parking lots or on Richard Estes' street corners. As his
introduction to the "new" postwar Germany, Abish's account is
painstakingly empirical.

> What are the first words a visitor from France can expect to hear
> upon his arrival at a German airport?
> Bonjour?
> Or, Guten Tag?

Or, Passport bitte? (P. 1)

And what is the first thing such a visitor might notice? Here is what the new German surface, remade since the war, asks one to note.

> Undoubtedly the cleanliness. The painstaking cleanliness. As well as the all-pervasive sense of order. A reassuring dependability. A punctuality. An almost obsessive punctuality. Then, of course, there is the new, striking architecture. Innovative? Hardly. Imaginative? Not really. But free of that former somber and authoritative massivity. A return to the experimentation of the Bauhaus? Regrettably no. Still, something must be said in favor of the wide expanse of glass on the buildings, the fifteen, twenty-story buildings, the glass reflecting not only the sky but also acting as a mirror for the older historical sites, those clutters of carefully reconstructed buildings that are an attempt to replicate entire neighborhoods obliterated in the last war. (Pp. 2–3).

This paragraph is almost self-consciously syntactical, with careful qualifications of each original detail much like Richard Estes sharpening the focus of a superrealistic painting. Following these initial qualifications come a series of adjectival questions answered by adverbs in a self-apparently parallel manner. Then for the paragraph's statement: that the key element is glass, one highly polished surface reflecting another (for as reconstructions, the historical sites can have no depth, only surface). Depth and meaning have been obliterated by something whose presence has now been entirely removed. Unlike the East, which leaves ruins as a memorial to and indictment of the wartime past, West Germany has tried to efface the war entirely, and what remains is a self-apparency of signs which mean only themselves.

Available form alternately expands and contracts meaning, Abish has argued. The topology of this new Germany makes the same point, for Abish's action takes place in a new, planned community, Brumholdstein, named after a Heidegger-like metaphysician whose specialty had been what makes "things" *things*. Brumholdstein is all surface, for it has been completed within the bounds (and maintained within the restoration budget for) a Nazi concentration camp. The city is built to the specifications of current need, with every detail worked out for the ideal population; but all these innovations must occur within the limits of the former camp.

The city's form, then, is self-evident—no illusions of random growth or of culture building through the ages. Brumholdstein is above all, like a Richard Estes or Ralph Goings canvas, an idea, a statement on the needs and fulfillments of life in postwar Germany as buildable within the boundaries it seeks to efface. Everywhere the past's temporal and spatial reality is present. Even the innocuous sentence, "The most glorious summer in thirty-four years," calls forth a calculation: 1978 minus 34 equals 1944, a very dark year the small-talking citizens would prefer to forget. A street caves in to reveal a mass grave. Certain persons hide uncertain pasts—was so-and-so a camp guard? Daughter of the commandant? Or perhaps a prisoner?

Abish's cast of characters live and build on this surface. Of the two Hargenau brothers, one works with steel and glass (as architect of the new municipal buildings), the other with words (as a novelist). The latter also has terrorist connections, a reference to those who would tear down what the former brother constructs over the war's ruins. To show the received quality of this life we are given a smart young couple, straight from the cover of *Stern*—Egon and Gisela, all glitter and surface, whose real life is a sickening morass of ego and autism. All is described in an austere, defamiliarized manner, almost as in a student's copybook. All hierarchal values are removed from Abish's perceptions, not so that we see the thing in itself (a *nouveau roman* attitude he satirizes through the philosopher Brumhold) but rather to emphasize the opaque nature of the sign. Once we humanize, Abish implies, we become subject to the same flawed rules of communication from which his characters suffer.

Besides the qualities of "all-over," "surface," and the like, there are more particular analogs to superrealism which indicate the special quality of experimental realism in fiction. Each genre wishes to emphasize sign over subject, and one way to accomplish this is to choose as image something wholly inappropriate to conventional art, so that the viewer-reader is discouraged from passing through the sign to a romanticized or idealized image of the actual thing. Here the superrealists are most characteristic, from Richard Estes' resistant facades to John Salt's junked cars resting in the weeds. Neither subject would be usable in any previous tradition of realism, and here the harsh window fronts and rusted-out autos remind one that there's more to the picture than *nature mort*; in effect the blinds are drawn on the signifier, arresting the viewer's vision at the canvas with the opacity of sign itself. Kenneth Gangemi's "Lydia" works much the same, as simple listing of a sixteen-year-old nymphet's venereal qualities—not for the implication of some Nabokovesque lyric but simply in and of themselves as outrageously unclean thoughts, yet so simple and direct that the reader is stuck on them as objects rather than passing through them to the forbidden territory of teen-age sex. Moreover, these signs are removed from context: we have no idea what's around the corner from Estes' drugstore or what Lydia may do later in the day. There is no meaning, no story; rather we are given a syntax of signs, as in the mix of pickup trucks in a Ralph Goings parking lot or the combination of car, trailer, and junk in a scene by John Salt. Above all, the painter or writer has no involvement with the scene, for all selection and framing has been taken care of by the photograph. With that out of the way, both creator and viewer are free to deal with the purely artistic problems of execution and reception—and these on the level of sign.

Flatness of sign is also important, for when dealing with an icon there's no need for anything else to be said. As if a picture can be worth a thousand words, Ken Gangemi writes his *Interceptor Pilot*[12] as a purely visual treatment: copy of *Le Monde* tossed on the journalist's car seat, two columns of smoke rising from the crash scene in the jungle. Here we have pure narrative, ignoring everything except what can be seen, which is another way of avoiding contamination of sign by reality. Peter Handke writes with a similarly visual sense, finding a narrative in which a character is so alienated from life that all he can do is rehearse the semiotic process, as in the following scene from *The Goalie's Anxiety at the Penalty Kick*.[13]

> Bloch was irritated. Within the segments themselves he saw the details with grating distinctness: as if the parts he saw stood for the whole. Again the details seemed to him like nameplates. "Neon signs," he thought. So he saw the waitress's ear with one earring as a sign of the entire person; and a purse on a nearby table, slightly open so that he could recognize a polka-dotted scarf in it, stood for the woman holding the coffee cup who sat behind it and, with her other hand, pausing only now and then at a picture, rapidly leafed through a magazine. A tower of ice-cream dishes dovetailed into each other on the bar seemed a simile for the café owner, and the puddle on the floor by the coat rack represented the umbrella hanging above it. Instead of the heads of the customers, Bloch saw the dirty spots on the wall at the level of their heads. (P. 88)

Handke's meditation on his mother's suicide, *A Sorrow Beyond Dreams*,[14] uses a similar sense of signs to show not only how a character can become caught up within the semiotics of her world but be defined by it as well:

> the GOOD OLD ironing board, the COZY hearth, the often-mended cooking pots, the DANGEROUS poker, the STURDY wheelbarrow, the ENTERPRISING weed cutter, the SHINING BRIGHT knives, which over the years had been ground to a vanishing narrowness by BURLEY scissors grinders, the FIENDISH thimble, the STUPID darning egg, the CLUMSY OLD flatiron, which provided variety by having to be put back on the stove every so often, and finally the PRIZE PIECE, the foot and hand-operated Singer sewing machine. (Pp. 41–42)

Handke needs the signs themselves, rather than what they refer to, for "words convey this sort of passive, complacent disgust much better than the sight of the phenomena they refer to" (p. 39). As far as a mother's life, "in the midst of these consoling fetishes, you ceased to exist. And because your days were spent in unchanging association with the same things, they became sacred to you" (p. 34). These are not "facts" but rather "the already available formulations, the linguistic deposit of man's social experience" (p. 29); for the young girls of the village, they become as hopscotch positions: Tired / Exhausted / Sick / Dying / Dead, "the stations in a woman's life" (p. 10). Her death and funeral are simply one more piece of generative grammar, as "only her name had to be inserted in the religious formulas" (p. 65).

What Handke describes is metonymy over metaphor, in which the concrete presence of a part of a thing works as sign for the rest, as opposed to the fluid transaction which takes place in metaphor. What has been produced is not a picture of objects, but a picture of a picture, much as the superrealistic painters produce: in this manner the photography or syntactically real sentence becomes part of the larger whole. Kenneth Gangemi loves to collect sentences which stand out as found objects, bizarrely turned phrases or ideas which draw more attention to themselves than to what they represent. "Who filled the cello with jello?" is one of these; another is "I once heard an American woman in the Hong Kong Hilton say 'Let's go to Chinatown'"; one can even make lists of zany ideas, such as "He rose quickly to the top of the shipping industry. He was the first to see that ships with cargoes of ping-pong balls did not have to carry insurance, since they could not sink anyway."

Cleansed of their nonsense, Gangemi's ditties could be considered reports from the world, and therefore part of history. The most extreme test for self-apparent fiction as it experiments with realism is to face history itself squarely, challenging image to dictate matter. The master of this technique is Guy Davenport, who has written stories using such recognizable characters as Edgar Allan Poe, Gertrude Stein, Picasso, and the Russian revolutionary artist Tatlin. In his work there is a careful shift from the camera-view of events so that the activity of fiction may take place. "My Tatlin is not Tatlin, nor my Poe Poe," Davenport insists. "But my stories are stories about them,"[15] just as the superrealists paint pictures of pictures. Once transformed, the historical image is something else, "a dream that strays into innocent sleep," Davenport says within his "necessary fictions," and "the mind is what it knows." Therefore he creates imaginative exercises on characters who are within the knowable past but who do not match up with our memory of it. Leonardo inventing a bicycle on which lancers will ride into battle full tilt; Gertrude Stein reading Picasso the Sunday comics; Greek philosophers inventing, in all seriousness, a mechanical pigeon; Richard Nixon bombing the DMZ to impress Chairman Mao, his host— like Kafka taking in the airshow at Brescia and brushing shoulders with Wittgenstein, these startling juxtapositions indicate the way our imaginations create the world, for the encounters Davenport presents seem so necessarily real.

Several of these stories, pertinently enough, use the chance of photography to make Davenport's point: Lenin snapped at a Zurich cafe while in the background James and Nora Joyce haggle with a taxi driver, a paleolithic fossil at the Museum of Natural History captured in an early experimental daguerreotype where a bystander, Edgar Allan Poe, is incorporated for scale. Why photography? Because "for the first time in the history of art the accidental becomes the controlling iconography of a representation of the world"[16] and hence a perfect analog for the human imagination at work in the creation of our world.

We know reality only through our fictions, which is the task experimental realism takes upon itself anew. In its process, the full range of techniques from self-apparent fiction are incorporated into the rediscovery of life itself, the noblest role for literary art and the surest way for fiction to be something added to the world and therefore important in itself. Reminding readers that fictions are provisional realities and not bedrock truth is the essence of self-apparent writing. Humans create their own meanings—in religions and in novels, each of which must remain properly *fictional* for the magic to work. Meaning resides not in the content of a novel or in a religion's material belief, but rather in the business of setting those things up. The content is not to be taken seriously—otherwise it becomes the stuff of great mischief, as fictional characters are gossiped about like scandalous neighbors and holy wars are waged over what were originally meant to be harmless rituals. Even worse from an aesthetic point of view, once the materials of novels or religions are taken as the one and only truth, their art evaporates to leave us with content alone, which deteriorates into just that much unformed chaos from our quotidian lives. But by discarding realist assumptions, the best of realistic conventions are saved, and both fiction and its surrounding culture live again.

Let's conclude with the convention of conclusions themselves. As a hallmark of Aristotelian form, endings are meant to be summations, resolutions, terminations of those developing actions which have brought the story to this point; endings are, in other words, *final*. But is there any way experimental realism can improve upon this oldest and most natural of conventions? As part of Stephen Dixon's work-in-progress titled *Time To Go*, which is itself a book of departures, the story "Goodbye to Goodbye" begins where many fictions end—"'Goodbye,' and she goes"—and hence must justify its continued existence by achieving a new sense of finality. Realizing that an ending is itself merely a convention whose artifice is not beyond experiment, Dixon tells one story of a potential conclusion thwarted by an heroic act: finding a rival boyfriend at his lover's apartment, the protagonist throws the guy out and impresses the girl friend anew. "That's not the way it happened, of course," Dixon adds after the first apparent ending, however, and retells the story with a few details made different. "That's not the way it happened either," he adds again, now making the girl friend a wife, adding a child to the cast of characters, and getting rid of the rival friend, all as a way of making her denial of love more pathetic and harder to bear. However, the protagonist once more asserts his love and wins her back. "That's ridiculous also and never happened," he admits, and spins one more tale of a broken love affair, this time salvaged only by the most extraordinary of means. In fifteen pages there have been three successively less reliable versions in which the one constant is a breakup narrowly averted at the last moment. And still, "That's not it. This is it," so once more the reader is treated to the familiar story, only now stripped of its more exotic details. "The marriage isn't working out" remains as the strongest sentence—by itself hardly worth a story, but thanks to Dixon's repeated modifications of the story's ending now sufficiently impressive in its sense of utter finality, which for eighteen pages has been almost hysterically resisted. When in the story's last line the door closes, we know that there can be no more retractions or revisions. This is definitely the end.

NOTES
INDEX

NOTES

Chapter 1. Introduction

1. In manuscript at this writing. Quotations, indicated parenthetically, are taken from the novel's first chapter as it appears in *SubStance*, Nos. 37 / 38 (1983), pp. 7–27.

2. E. L. Doctorow, *Ragtime* (New York: Random House, 1975).

3. Ishmael Reed, *Yellow Back Radio Broke Down* (Garden City, N.Y.: Doubleday, 1969).

4. Steve Katz. *Moving Parts* (New York: Fiction Collective, 1977). Each of this book's four sections is paginated independently.

5. Donald Barthelme, "Me and Miss Mandible," *Come Back, Dr. Caligari* (Boston: Little, Brown, 1964), pp. 95–111. Barthelme's first published story, it originally appeared as "The Darling Duckling at School" in *Contact*, No. 7 (Feb. 1961), pp. 17–28.

6. These developments are studied in my *The American 1960s* (Ames: Iowa State Univ. Press, 1980) and *Literary Disruptions* (Urbana: Univ. of Illinois Press, 1975; revised and expanded, 1980).

Chapter 2. The Self-Effacing Word

1. Philip Roth, *Goodbye, Columbus* (Boston: Houghton Mifflin, 1959).

2. Kurt Vonnegut, Jr., "The Hyannis Port Story," *Welcome to the Monkey House* (New York: Delacorte Press / Seymour Lawrence, 1968), pp. 133–45. This is the story's first publication, having been sold to the *Saturday Evening Post* but not run because of the presidential assassination.

3. Roman Jakobson, "Qu'est-ce que la poésie," in *Questions de poétique*, ed. Tzvetan Todorov (Paris: Seuil, 1973), p. 124.

4. Roman Jakobson, "Linguistics and Poetics," in *Style in Language*, ed. Thomas Sebeok (Cambridge: MIT Press, 1960), p. 358.

5. Hughes Rudd, "Miss Euayla is the Sweetest *Thang!*", *Paris Review*, No. 26 (1961), pp. 13–27.

6. Bernard Malamud, "The Jewbird," *Idiots First* (New York: Farrar, Straus & Giroux, 1963), pp. 101–13.

7. Donald Barthelme, "Porcupines at the University," *New Yorker*, 46 (Apr. 25, 1970), 32–33.

8. Richard Schickel, "Freaked Out on Barthelme," *New York Times Magazine*, Aug. 16, 1970, p. 15.

9. Jerome Klinkowitz, "Donald Barthelme: An Interview," in *The New Fiction: Interviews with Innovative American Writers*, ed. Joe David Bellamy (Urbana: Univ. of Illinois Press, 1974), p. 25.

10. Donald Barthelme, comments on "Paraguay," in *Writer's Choice*, ed. Rust Hills (New York: David McKay, 1974), p. 25.

11. Donald Barthelme et al., "A Symposium on Fiction," *Shenandoah*, 27 (Winter 1976), 20–21.

12. Richard Brautigan, *Trout Fishing in America* (San Francisco: Four Seasons Foundation, 1967).

13. Robert Coover, *The Origin of the Brunists* (New York: Putnam's, 1966).

14. Robert Coover, *The Universal Baseball Association, J. Henry Waugh, Prop.* (New York: Random House, 1968).

15. Robert Coover, *The Public Burning* (New York: Viking Press, 1977).

16. Robert Coover, "The Public Burning of Julius and Ethel Rosenberg: An Historical Romance," *TriQuarterly*, No. 26 (Winter 1973), pp. 268–69. This excerpt from the novel then in progress is cited for virtue of its conciseness.

17. Robert Coover, "The Babysitter," *Pricksongs and Descants* (New York: Dutton, 1969), pp. 206–39.

18. Ronald Sukenick, "Momentum," *The Death of the Novel and Other Stories* (New York: Dial Press, 1969), pp. 9–40.

Chapter 3. Strategies Against Effacement

1. William York Tindall, *A Reader's Guide to James Joyce* (New York: Farrar, Straus & Giroux, 1959), p. 125.

2. Richard Kostelanetz, ed., *The Yale Gertrude Stein* (New Haven: Yale Univ. Press, 1980 , p. xiv.

3. William S. Burroughs, "Letter from a Master Addict to Dangerous Drugs," *British Journal of Addiction*, 53, No. 2; reprinted as an appendix to *Naked Lunch* (New York: Grove Press, 1959), p. 242.

4. Daniel Odier, *The Job: Interviews with William S. Burroughs* (New York: Grove Press, 1970), p. 13.

5. William S. Burroughs and Brion Gysin, *The Third Mind* (New York: Viking Press, 1978), p. 2; roots of the cut-up technique are discussed in *The Job*, pp. 14–22.

6. Steven G. Kellman, *The Self-Begetting Novel* (New York: Columbia Univ. Press, 1980), p. 3.

7. Ronald Barthes, *Writing Degree Zero*, trans. Annette Lavers and Colin Smith (Boston: Beacon Press, 1970), pp. 2–3; first published as *Le Degré zéro de l'écriture* (Paris; Seuil, 1953).

8. Alain Robbe-Grillet, "Order and Disorder in Contemporary Fiction," *New Orleans Review*, 6, No. 1 (1979), 19 (trans. Joseph LaCour).

9. Stephen Heath, *The Nouveau Roman* (London: Paul Elek, 1972; Philadelphia: Temple Univ. Press, 1972), p. 68.

10. Alain Robbe-Grillet, *For a New Novel*, trans. Richard Howard (New York: Grove Press, 1965), p. 72; first published as *Pour un nouveau roman* (Paris: Minuit, 1963).

11. Roland Barthes, *Critical Essays*, trans. Richard Howard (Evanston, Ill.: Northwestern Univ. Press, 1972), p. 5; first published as *Essais critiques* (Paris: Seuil, 1964).

12. Alain Robbe-Grillet, "Introduction," *Last Year at Marienbad*, trans. Richard Howard (New York: Grove Press, 1962), p. 7; first published as *L'Année dernière á Marienbad* (Paris: Minuit, 1961).

13. Jacques Derrida, *Speech and Phenomena and Other Essays on Husserl's Theory of Signs*, trans. David B. Allison (Evanston, Ill.: Northwestern Univ. Press, 1973), p. 99; first published as *La Voix et la phénomène* (Paris: Presses Universitaries de France, 1967).

14. Jonathan Culler, *Structuralist Poetics* (London, Routledge & Keegan Paul, 1975; Ithaca, N.Y.: Cornell Univ. Press, 1975), p. 5.

15. Jonathan Culler, "Semiotics and Deconstruction," *Poetics Today*, 1 (Autumn 1979), 138.

16. "Translator's Preface" to Jacques Derrida, *Of Grammatology*, trans. Gayatri Chakravorty Spivak (Baltimore: Johns Hopkins Univ. Press, 1976), p. xvii; Derrida's book itself was first published as *De la grammatologie* (Paris: Minuit, 1967).

17. Richard Rorty, "Philosophy as a Kind of Writing: An Essay on Derrida," *New Literary History*, 10 (Autumn 1978), 153.

18. Jacques Derrida, *Writing and Difference*, trans. Alan Bass (Chicago: Univ. of Chicago Press, 1978), p. 5; first published as *L'Ecriture et la différence* (Paris: Seuil, 1967).

19. Philip Roth, "Writing American Fiction," *Commentary*, 31 (Mar. 1961), 224; collected in Roth's *Reading Myself and Others* (New York: Farrar, Straus & Giroux, 1975), p. 120.

20. Julia Kristeva, *Desire in Language*, trans. Leon Roudiez et al. (New York: Columbia Univ. Press, 1980), pp. 70–71; the essay quoted first appeared in her book *Semiotika* (Paris: Seuil, 1969).

21. Douglas R. Hofstadter, "Metamagical Themas," *Scientific American*, 244 (Jan. 1981), 22, 24, 27–28, 30, 32.

22. Philippe Sollers, *Logiques* (Paris: Seuil, 1968), p. 238 (my translation).

Chapter 4. Reflexive Fiction

1. Samuel Beckett, "Dante . . . Bruno. Vico . . Joyce," in *I Can't Go On. I'll Go On*, ed. Richard Seaver (New York: Grove Press, 1976), p. 117. First published in 1929.

2. Donald Barthelme, "After Joyce," *Location*, No. 1 (Summer 1964), p. 13.

3. Anaïs Nin, *The Novel of the Future* (New York: Macmillan, 1968), p. 25.

4. William H. Gass, *Fiction and the Figures of Life* (New York: Knopf, 1970), p. 27.

5. M. M. Bakhtin, *The Dialogic Imagination* (Austin: Univ. of Texas Press, 1981), p. 51.

6. Richard Brautigan, *Trout Fishing in America* (San Francisco: Four Seasons Foundation, 1967), p. 20.

7. Tom Robbins, *Another Roadside Attraction* (New York: Doubleday, 1971), p. 89.

8. John Gardner, *On Moral Fiction* (New York: Basic Books, 1978).

9. Gerald Graff, *Literature Against Itself* (Chicago: Univ. of Chicago Press, 1979).

10. Gerald Graff, "Responses and Discussion," *Bulletin of the Midwest Modern Language Association*, 13 (Spring 1980), 11.

11. Frank D. McConnell, *Four Postwar American Novelists* (Chicago: Univ. of Chicago Press, 1977), pp. xvi–xvii.

12. Josephine Hendin, *Vulnerable People: A View of American Fiction Since 1945* (New York: Oxford Univ. Press, 1978), p. 225.

13. Mas'ud Zavarzadeh, *The Mythopoeic Reality* (Urbana: Univ. of Illinois Press, 1976), p. 222.

14. Gilbert Sorrentino, "'The Various Isolated': W. C. Williams' Prose," *New American Review*, No. 15 (1972), p. 195.

15. Ronald Sukenick, "Twelve Digressions Toward a Theory of Composition," *New Literary History*, 6 (Winter 1974–75), 429–37; "Thirteen Digressions," *Partisan Review*, 43, No. 1 (1976), 90–101; "Fiction in the Seventies:

Ten Digressions on Ten Digressions," *Studies in American Fiction*, 5 (Spring 1977), 99–108; "Eight Digressions on the Politics of Language," *New Literary History*, 11 (Spring 1979), 467–77.

16. Gerald Graff, "Response [to Hans-Georg Gadamer]," *Bulletin of the Midwest Modern Language Association*, 13 (Spring 1980), 11.

17. Donald Barthelme, "Marie, Marie, Hold on Tight," *New Yorker*, 39 (Oct. 12, 1963), 49–51; "The Darling Duckling at School," *Contact*, No. 7 (Feb. 1961), pp. 17–28, collected and retitled "Me and Miss Mandible" in *Come Back, Dr. Caligari* (Boston: Little, Brown, 1964), pp. 97–111; "Man's Face," *New Yorker*, 40 (May 30, 1964), 29.

18. Donald Barthelme, "Sentence," *New Yorker*, 45 (Mar. 7, 1970), 34–36; collected in *City Life* (New York: Farrar, Straus & Giroux, 1970), pp. 105–14.

19. Donald Barthelme, "Mouth," *Paris Review*, No. 48 (Fall 1969), pp. 189–202; retitled "Bone Bubbles" and collected in *City Life*, pp. 115–24.

20. "Paraguay," *New Yorker*, 45 (Sept. 6, 1969), 32–34; collected in *City Life*, pp. 17–27.

21. Donald Barthelme, commentary on "Paraguay," in *Writer's Choice*, ed. Rust Hills (New York: McKay, 1974), p. 25.

22. Donald Barthelme et al., "A Symposium on Fiction," *Shenandoah*, 27 (Winter 1976), 20–21.

23. Jerome Klinkowitz, "Interview with Donald Barthelme," in *The New Fiction*, ed. Joe David Bellamy (Urbana: Univ. of Illinois Press, 1974), p. 48.

24. Donald Barthelme, "A Nation of Wheels," *New Yorker*, 46 (June 13, 1970), 36–39; collected in *Guilty Pleasures* (New York: Farrar, Straus & Giroux, 1974), pp. 135–45.

25. Donald Barthelme, "Momma," *New Yorker*, 54 (Oct. 2, 1978), 29–30; combined with "The New Music" and collected under that title in *Great Days* (New York: Farrar, Straus & Giroux, 1979), pp. 21–38.

26. Donald Barthelme, "Porcupines at the University," *New Yorker*, 46 (Apr. 25, 1970), 32–33; collected in *Amateurs* (New York: Farrar, Straus & Giroux, 1976), pp. 115–21.

27. Donald Barthelme, introduction to *Here in the Village* (Northridge, Calif.: Lord John Press, 1978), p. 9.

28. William H. Gass, *Willie Masters' Lonesome Wife* (Evanston, Ill.: Tri-Quarterly Supplement no. 2, 1968), unpaged.

29. William H. Gass, *On Being Blue* (Boston: David R. Godine, 1976), p. 18.

30. Ronald Sukenick, *Up* (New York: Dial Press, 1968).

31. Ronald Sukenick, *Wallace Stevens, Musing the Obscure* (New York: New York Univ. Press, 1967), pp. 14–15.

32. Ronald Sukenick, *The Death of the Novel and Other Stories* (New York: Dial Press, 1969).

Chapter 5. The Self-Apparent Word

1. Walter Abish, "The Writer-To-Be: An Impression of Living," *SubStance*, No. 27 (Winter 1980–81), p. 103.

2. Abish's paper was presented at the international conference, "Innovation and Renovation in Western Culture," organized at the Wingspread Conference Center and the University of Wisconsin-Milwaukee in September, 1981, by Ihab Hassan.

3. Walter Abish, *How German Is It* (New York: New Directions, 1980).

4. Walter Abish, "Self-Portrait," in *Individuals: Post-Movement Art in America*, ed. Alan Sondheim (New York: Dutton, 1977), pp. 1–25.

5. Walter Abish, *Minds Meet* (New York: New Directions: 1975.

6. In the original manuscript later changed for publication by *Seems* magazine, Abish named his character Jean-Luc Godard.

7. Walter Abish, *In the Future Perfect* (New York: New Directions, 1977).

8. Walter Abish, "Inside Out," *Personal Injury*, No. 4 (1977), pp. 57–68.

9. Walter Abish, "Ninety-Nine: The New Meaning," *Renegade*, No. 1 (1979), pp. 2–15.

10. Walter Abish, "What Else," *Conjunctions*, No. 1 (Winter 1981–82), pp. 105–19.

11. Stephen Dixon, *14 Stories* (Baltimore: Johns Hopkins Univ. Press, 1980).

12. Stephen Dixon, *No Relief* (Ann Arbor: Street Fiction Press, 1976).

13. Stephen Dixon, *Work* (Ann Arbor: Street Fiction Press, 1977).

14. Stephen Dixon, *Too Late* (New York: Harper & Row, 1978).

15. Stephen Dixon, *Quite Contrary: The Mary and Newt Story* (New York: Harper & Row, 1979).

16. Stephen Dixon, *Movies* (San Francisco: North Point Press, 1983).

17. Stephen Dixon, *Love and Will* (in manuscript at this writing).

18. Stephen Dixon, *Time to Go* (in manuscript at this writing, scheduled for 1984 publication by the Johns Hopkins Univ. Press, Baltimore).

19. Stephen Dixon, "Time to Go," quoted from its first serial publication in *TriQuarterly*, No. 56 (Winter 1983), p. 223.

20. Clarence Major, *Reflex and Bone Structure* (New York: Fiction Collective, 1975).

21. Tzvetan Todorov, *The Poetics of Prose*, trans. Richard Howard (Ithaca, N.Y.: Cornell Univ. Press, 1977), p. 45. Orginally published as *La Poetique de la prose* (Paris: Seuil, 1971).

22. Clarence Major, *Emergency Exit* (New York: Fiction Collective, 1979).

23. John O'Brien, *Interviews with Black Writers* (New York: Liveright, 1973), p. 130.

Chapter 6. Experimental Realism

1. Stephen Dixon, "Said," *Boundary* 2, 8 (Spring 1980), 99–100.
2. Jerome Klinkowitz, "Interview with Walter Abish," *Fiction International* Nos. 4 / 5 (Fall 1975), p. 95.
3. Kenneth Gangemi, *Olt* (New York: Orion Press, 1969), pp. 49–50.
4. Howard McCord, "The Geography of Ohio," *Fiction International*, Nos. 2 / 3 (Fall 1974), p. 121.
5. Leonard Michaels, "In the Fifties," *I Would Have Saved Them If I Could* (New York: Farrar, Straus & Giroux, 1975), pp. 59–60.
6. Gilbert Sorrentino, *Splendide-Hotel* (New York: New Directions, 1973), p. 13.
7. Philip Stevick, *Alternative Pleasures* (Urbana: Univ. of Illinois Press, 1981), p. 103.
8. Gilles Deleuze, *Proust and Signs*, trans. Richard Howard (New York: Braziller, 1972), p. 26. Originally published as *Proust et les signes* (Paris: Presses Universitaires de France, 1964).
9. Walter Abish, "This Is Not A Film. This Is A Precise Act Of Disbelief," *Minds Meet* (New York: New Directions, 1975), p. 31.
10. Abish interview, p. 96.
11. Walter Abish, *How German Is It* (New York: New Directions, 1980).
12. Kenneth Gangemi, *The Interceptor Pilot* (London: Marion Boyars, 1980); originally published in a translation by Samantha Martin and Livia Standersi as *Pilot de chasse* (Paris: Flammarion, 1974).
13. Peter Handke, *The Goalie's Anxiety at the Penalty Kick*, trans. Ralph Mannheim (New York: Farrar, Straus & Giroux, 1972); originally published as *Die Angst des Tormanns beim Elfmeter* (Frankfurt: Suhrkamp, 1970).
14. Peter Handke, *A Sorrow Beyond Dreams*, trans. Ralph Mannheim (New York: Farrar, Straus & Giroux, 1975); originally published as *Wunschloses Unglück* (Salzburg: Residenz Verlag, 1972).
15. Guy Davenport, "Ernst Mach Max Ernst," *The Geography of the Imagination* (San Francisco: North Point Press, 1981), p. 383.
16. Guy Davenport, "The Invention of Photography in Toledo," *Da Vinci's Bicycle* (Baltimore: Johns Hopkins Univ. Press, 1979), p. 123.

INDEX